you & your wedding

WEDDING VOWS READINGS & MUSIC

you & your wedding

WEDDING VOWS READINGS & MUSIC

Carole Hamilton

illustrations by Max Savva

foulsham
LONDON • NEW YORK • TORONTO • SYDNEY

foulsham

The Oriel
Thames Valley Court
183–187 Bath Road
Slough
Berkshire SL1 4AA
England

you & your wedding

For Nick and George

Foulsham books can be found in all good bookshops and direct from www.foulsham.com

ISBN: 978-0-572-03570-9

Copyright © 2007 The National Magazine Company Limited
The expression You & Your Wedding is a registered trademark of The National Magazine Company.
Copyright of the book illustrations belongs to The National Magazine Company Limited
Cover illustration © The National Magazine Company Limited
A CIP record for this book is available from the British Library
Carole Hamilton has asserted her moral right to be identified as the author of this work

All rights reserved

Other books in this series:
The Groom's Guide (978-0-572-03265-4)
The Bride's Book (978-0-572-03316-3)
The Best Man's Book (978-0-572-03366-8)
The Wedding Planner (978-0-572-03345-3)

The Copyright Act prohibits (subject to certain very limited exceptions) the making of copies of any copyright work or of a substantial part of such a work, including the making of copies by photocopying or similar process. Written permission to make a copy or copies must therefore normally be obtained from the publisher in advance. It is advisable also to consult the publisher if in any doubt as to the legality of any copying which is to be undertaken.

While every effort has been made to ensure the accuracy of all the information contained within this book, neither the author nor the publisher can be liable for any errors. In particular, since laws change from time to time, it is vital that each individual checks relevant legal details for themselves.

Every effort has been made to contact copyright holders of the extracts included in this book. Where it has not been possible to trace any copyright holder, despite our best endeavours, we would ask that anyone claiming such copyright should contact the publishers with full details, and if an author's copyright has been inadvertently infringed sincere apologies are tendered.

Printed in Dubai

Design: Matthew Inman at www.spinning-top.com
Illustrations: Max Savva at www.spinning-top.com

Contents

1 Where to find the right words.................... 8
Where to start your search for the right words to include in both religious and civil ceremonies

2 The vows of marriage 16
Ideas for traditional vows, as well as inspiration for writing words that are all your own

3 All about wedding readings........................ 32
Where and what to include in your order of service, plus whom to choose to give your readings

4 Readings for a civil ceremony 38
Inspiration from the traditional to the thoroughly modern

5 Readings for a religious ceremony.............. 84
Sample texts suitable for a traditional wedding, plus prayers and blessings

6 Ceremony hymns and wedding music....... 128
The music to choose for the moment you walk up the aisle through to your first dance as man and wife

7 Wedding speeches and toasts 146
Guidelines for anyone making a speech, plus sample celebratory toasts

Acknowledgements 172
Index 173

The
moment
you
say 'I do'

Introduction

As editor of *You & Your Wedding* magazine, I met hundreds of couples as they embarked on the adventure of getting married. They were always full of excitement about the venue, the dress and the food… the one thing that was rarely mentioned was the ceremony, which is strange since this is what getting married is all about!

What you say to one another as you make the all-important commitment of marriage, as well as the choice of readings and music at the ceremony, plays a big part in creating a memorable occasion for both of you, as well as your friends and family. So I think it deserves more than a few minutes' thought in the whirlwind of planning everything else, which is why I have written this book.

Whether you are having a religious or a civil ceremony, I hope that you will gain inspiration and guidance in the following chapters. You will find advice on planning your ceremony as well as masses of favourite readings from the traditional to the modern. There are also musical ideas for each section of the ceremony.

The marriage ceremony shouldn't be viewed as something to get out of the way so the party can get started and if you don't give it much thought, I think you might regret it later. Take a moment now to reflect on the addition of a few meaningful moments, and the tears in the eyes of the congregation as you become husband and wife will definitely be worth the effort. Have a wonderful wedding!

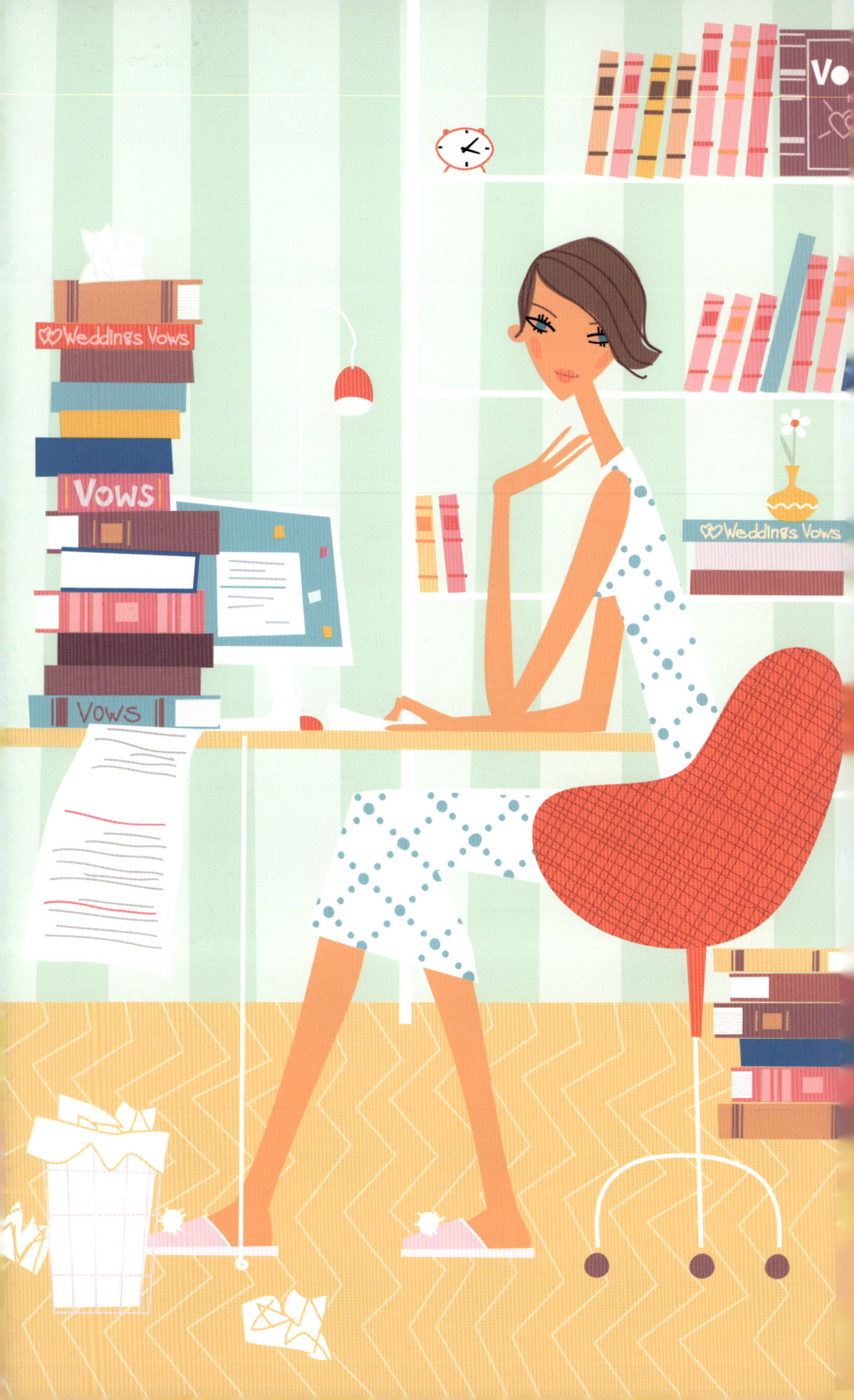
Weddings Vows
Vows
Vows
Weddings Vows
Vo

Chapter 1

Where to find the right words

The marriage ceremony is much more than just saying 'I do'. The perfect ceremony is a carefully chosen balance between words and music that are meaningful to the bride and groom and memorable for all the guests.

Organising a wedding is a whirlwind of arrangements, decisions and spending money. The thing that often slips to the bottom of the list of priorities is the ceremony, which is actually the whole point of getting married in the first place, so is crucial to the success of the whole event!

You don't have to say much at all to become legally married. It is basically the bride and groom giving consent to marry in front of an officiant: 'Do you, John, take Jane to be your lawfully wedded wife?' 'I do' (and vice versa). But surely this isn't what all the waiting and anticipation has been about?

Agreeing to become man and wife is a big commitment, a public declaration of your love and fidelity in front of family and friends, and what you say to one another really does matter. The words and music that you include in your order of service – whether it is a religious or civil wedding – need to be carefully considered, and it all deserves more than a few minutes of your time.

This book will help to guide you through making the right choices as you start to plan your perfect day.

The order of service

The order of service is the 'running order' of the wedding ceremony, with the vows forming the central part of the event. It is much the same at any wedding, although it's usually simplified if you are having a civil ceremony. Think about each section and the mood you want to achieve as you decide on the appropriate content.

Prelude: The wedding party and guests arrive and are seated to soothing music, usually played by an organist or a string quartet.

Processional: The congregation stand as the bride arrives and makes her way down the aisle to some suitably triumphant or romantic music.

Welcome: The officiant welcomes the congregation as the bride and groom are joined in matrimony. At a religious wedding there is usually a blessing.

Consent: The bride and groom will be asked if they are free to marry and those present asked if they know of any reason why the marriage may not take place.

Readings: Short readings or musical interludes form part of most ceremonies and can be added in several slots throughout the service.

Exchange of vows: Personal words exchanged by the bride and groom.

Exchange of rings: The bride and groom exchange rings. At a religious ceremony the officiant will bless the rings.

Signing the register: The bride, groom and two witnesses sign the register.

Closing remarks: The officiant brings the ceremony to a close and the bride and groom are declared husband and wife. The happy couple kiss and the congregation may applaud.

Recessional: The recessional music – which usually has a suitably 'loved up' theme – begins, and the couple walk back down the aisle.

Where to find the right words

The order of service is printed at the same time as any stationery for the reception and a copy given to each of the guests so that they can follow the proceedings. The words of any readings and hymns are often included, as well as the name of the officiant, the organist, any other musicians and anyone giving a reading. At a traditional ceremony, the ushers are responsible for distributing the order of service, handing one to each guest or placing one on each seat.

If you want to include the words to any hymns or readings, check with your officiant whether you need copyright clearance to reprint these. If you do, it usually only involves paying a small fee (£15–£25) and he or she will have the details of how this is done. Printing the words of hymns is a good idea if you want everyone to join in and it prevents guests having to search through a hymn book.

Marriage legalities
To be legally married in the UK you need to comply with these rules:

- You and your fiancé must be at least 16 years old. (In England, Wales and Northern Ireland, if either of you is under 18, one parent or guardian must give consent.)
- You must not be closely related.
- In England, Wales and Northern Ireland, the marriage must take place in premises where the ceremony can be legally solemnised (register office, premises licensed for marriage, or a parish church or other place of worship registered for marriage). In Scotland you can marry anywhere, providing a minister and witnesses are present.
- The ceremony must take place in the presence of a registrar or another authorised person, such as a priest or rabbi.
- In England, Wales and Northern Ireland, the ceremony must take place between 8am and 6pm. In Scotland there are no time restrictions.
- Two witnesses must be present.
- You must both be free and eligible to marry.

The religious ceremony

Each faith has a slightly different marriage ceremony and you should talk through the wording with your officiant beforehand. This is your chance to think about what you want to say and if you would prefer to word things a little differently. For example, these days not many brides agree to 'obey' their groom as part of the ceremony and both the bride and the groom (it used to be just the groom) agree to share all their 'worldly goods'. It all depends on the views of the minister as to whether he or she will agree to your requests.

A religious ceremony doesn't offer as much scope as a civil ceremony for changing the wording, but some ministers or priests are happy to consider minor revisions if you have a good reason for wanting the changes.

The bride and groom traditionally face one another to say their vows, usually with their backs to the congregation, although a more modern approach is for the officiant to have his or her back to the congregation so the couple face forward, making the whole ceremony feel a little more personal.

The civil ceremony

If you don't want a religious ceremony or are prevented from doing so because of divorce or mixed faith, then the alternative is a civil wedding. You can choose from either a register office ceremony or one performed in a building that holds a marriage licence. In either case, the process for arranging everything is the same.

Firstly, you need to contact the superintendent registrar for your district, which you must have lived in for a minimum of seven days. Even if both of you live in the same district, each of you needs your own superintendent registrar's certificate, so both bride and groom must apply in person to the local office. You then wait 15 days for the certificate to be issued and this is valid for 12 months.

Use this first appointment to check that your preferred date is free and that a registrar is free to attend your venue, if you want to have a wedding in a licensed building. This is very important and you should never book your venue until you know that the registrar is able to marry you on a particular date. If you are marrying

Where to find the right words

out of your district, you'll need to speak to the superintendent registrar for the area you have chosen about booking a ceremony.

If you haven't yet decided on a venue, the registrar will be able to give you a list of local licensed premises. For a full list of over 3,000 licensed premises visit www.gro.gov.uk/gro/content/marriages, where you can search by area or buy a copy of the list for a small fee.

In a civil ceremony you have more scope to personalise proceedings, even going as far as writing your own vows. Just remember that this is still a legal ceremony and anything you want to include should reflect the solemnity of the occasion. Keep anything too personal for a private moment between the two of you. For examples of personalising your vows, see Chapter 2 The vows of marriage (page 25).

Legally, a civil wedding cannot contain vows, songs, poems or readings that have any religious references – and this can even mean words like 'angel' in some cases – so it's very important that you check everything you want to include with your registrar. Ideally, you should give them a typed version of what you intend to say and a list of any music at least two weeks before the wedding, to give you plenty of time to make any necessary amendments.

At a civil wedding you generally won't be able to extend the ceremony beyond a total of about 20 minutes, sometimes even shorter if you are having a register office ceremony.

The informal nature of the civil ceremony is what attracts many couples, but you should definitely think about adding a few readings or poems. Otherwise the whole thing could be over so quickly that your guests will hardly have taken their seats before you have said your vows and are man and wife. The speedy nature of the marriage ceremony has taken some couples unawares and you don't want it to feel like a non-event.

If you are marrying in licensed premises, the order of service can follow pretty much the same format as for a religious ceremony; it's just the words that are different and, of course, there are no hymns or prayers. A register office ceremony is usually much simpler, but most locations will have a CD player to play your favourite music as you come in and leave.

The humanist wedding

A humanist ceremony allows complete freedom to say what you like to each other, although it is not legally recognised in England, Wales or Northern Ireland so you will have to undertake a traditional civil ceremony first. It is legally recognised in Scotland. Humanists believe in human ethics without the need for religious authority, so a humanist wedding focuses on the couple's relationship and why they want to make a public declaration of their commitment.

Whatever type of marriage ceremony seems most appropriate to you, it's always a good idea to get some expert advice. Make an appointment to see your local minister, priest, rabbi or registrar and talk to them about what is involved. They will be only too happy to answer your questions about what is and isn't possible and how each service is structured.

The wedding abroad

If you are planning a wedding abroad, it is likely to be a civil ceremony, although it is possible to arrange for a religious ceremony in some countries or perhaps to have a church blessing after a civil ceremony.

The country you choose for your wedding will determine whether the ceremony is held in English. It usually will be, but in some parts of Italy, for example, the ceremony will be in Italian and since you need to understand the words you might need the services of an interpreter to make the ceremony run smoothly.

Find out exactly what is involved in the basic ceremony – and the wording of the marriage vows – from whoever is arranging the wedding for you. Once you know what format the traditional service will take, you can decide whether or not you want to add some words of your own. It's usually possible to tailor your vows for a

Where to find the right words

civil wedding abroad, although it is best to keep things simple. You will still need to seek approval of anything you want to add and it could all get complicated if your words are being translated into another language. As far as music is concerned, if there is a particular piece of music or a song that you would love to have playing in the background, take it with you on a disc and ask to borrow a portable CD player from the hotel. Wedding ceremonies in many countries are held outside and there may not be a chance to have any pre-recorded music, but you could organise a local band to join you, if you wish.

If you have managed to arrange a religious ceremony abroad, it is unlikely that you will be able to have any input into the service and will have to go along with whatever is traditional in that country.

Your ceremony - useful contacts list

For extra help and advice with every aspect of your ceremony:

Baptists' Union	01235 517700	www.baptist.org.uk
British Humanist Assoc.	020 7079 3580	www.humanism.org.uk
Catholic Church	020 7371 1341	www.marriagecare.org.uk
Church of England	020 7898 1000	www.cofe.anglican.org
Church of Scotland	01312 255722	www.churchofscotland.org.uk
General Register Office (GRO)		
for England and Wales	01514 714200	www.ons.gov.uk
GRO for Guernsey	01481 725277	
GRO for Jersey	01534 502335	
GRO for Northern Ireland	02890 252000	www.groni.gov.uk
GRO for Scotland	01313 144447	www.gro-scotland.gov.uk
Greek Archdiocese	020 7723 4787	www.thyateira.org.uk
Jewish Marriage Council	020 8203 6311	www.somethingjewish.co.uk
Methodist Church	020 7222 8010	www.methodist.org.uk
United Reform Church	020 7916 2020	www.urc.org.uk

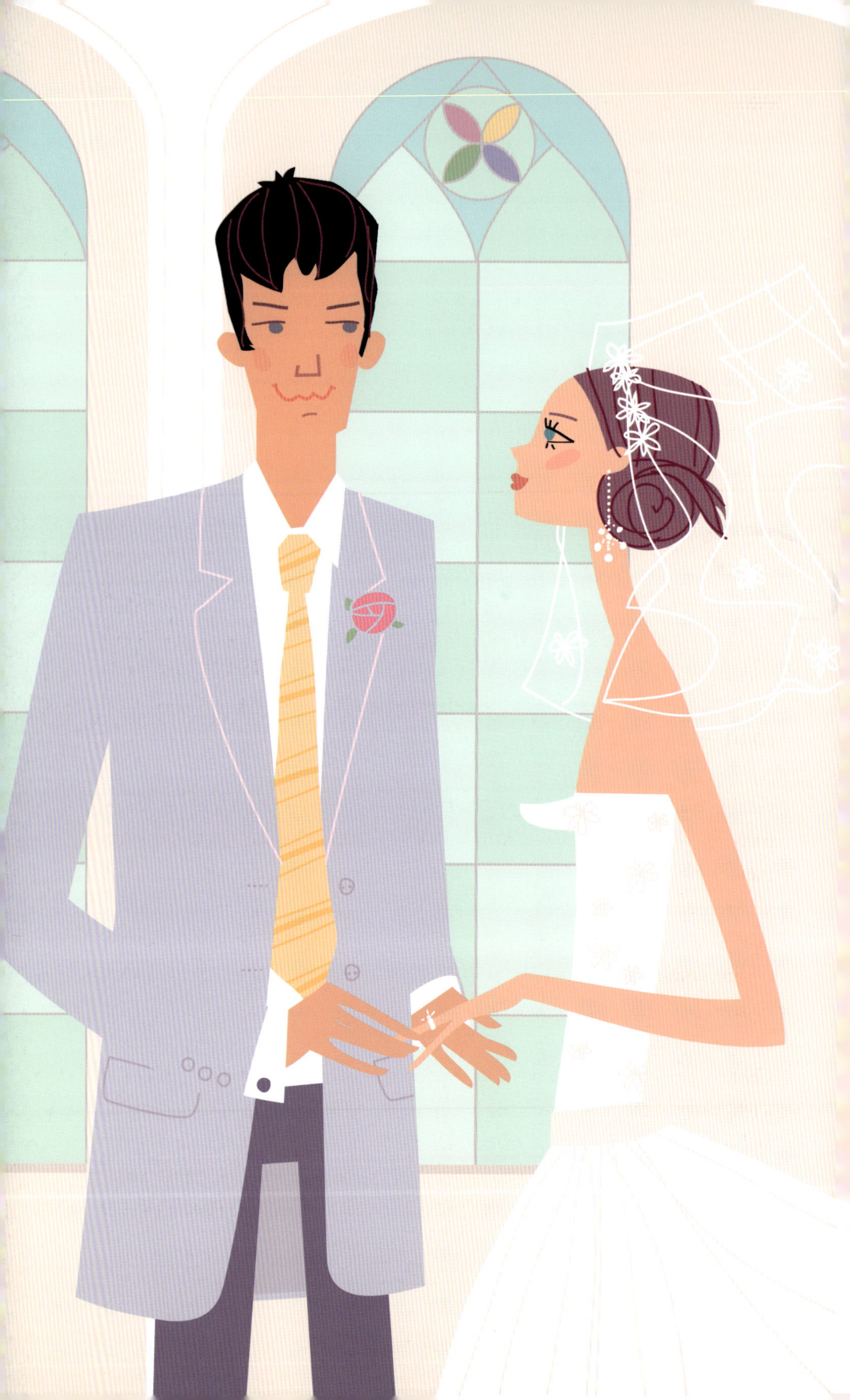

Chapter 2

The vows of marriage

The words you say to one another during the marriage ceremony should be heartfelt, regardless of whether you are having a religious or a civil ceremony. This is the big moment of commitment when you legally become man and wife.

Getting married is much more than wearing a gorgeous dress and enjoying a great party; you are agreeing to be legally bound in marriage to another person and this shouldn't be entered into lightly. All wedding vows are promises and you must not underestimate the power of the moment that you commit your future to another person. Whether you are having a religious or a civil ceremony, spend some time reading samples of traditional vows so that you are comfortable with what you will be saying when it comes to your big moment.

Civil ceremonies allow more room for personalising what you say, but even with a religious ceremony there is scope for minor changes. Sit down with one another and discuss whether you want to use traditional vows or add something of your own. But remember: it is important that any changes are checked with the officiant well in advance, as it can be the case that unexpected problems could arise if you have chosen to include something that is not acceptable.

Religious wedding vows

Different faiths have different versions of the marriage vows, but they are all broadly about making a public declaration that you are both free to be married, and then committing yourselves to be loving and faithful for the rest of your lives.

Here are the basic vows for many of the main faiths, most of which are based on the Protestant Book of Common Prayer. They are either a series of questions or statements to which the couple responds 'I do' or 'I will'.

Church of England vows

'I, ..., take thee, ..., to be my lawfully wedded wife/husband, to have and to hold, from this day forward, for better, for worse, for richer, for poorer, in sickness and in health, to love and to cherish 'til death do us part, according to God's holy ordinance, and thereto I pledge thee my troth/pledge myself to you.'

Roman Catholic vows

The Catholic marriage ceremony usually forms part of a full mass but you can choose a shorter service, particularly if either the bride or groom is not Catholic.

'I, ..., take you, ..., to be my wife/husband. I promise to be true to you in good times and in bad, in sickness and in health. I will love you and honour you all the days of my life.'

'I, ..., take you, ..., for my lawful wife/husband, to have and to hold from this day forward, for better, for worse, for richer, for poorer, in sickness and health, until death do us part.'

Baptist vows

'Will you, ..., have .... to be your wife/husband? Will you love her/him, comfort and keep her/him, and forsaking all others remain true to her/him as long as both shall live?'

'I, ..., take thee, ..., to be my wife/husband, and before God and these witnesses I promise to be a faithful and true husband/wife.'

The vows of marriage

Methodist vows

'Will you have this woman/man to be your wife/husband, to live together in a holy marriage? Will you love her/him, comfort her/him, honour and keep her/him in sickness and in health, and forsaking all others, be faithful to her/him as long as you shall live?'

'In the name of God, I, ………, take you, ………, to be my wife/husband, to have and to hold from this day forward, for better, for worse, for richer, for poorer, in sickness and in health, to love and to cherish, until we are parted by death. This is my solemn vow.'

Hindu vows

The traditional Hindu ceremony is a complicated affair involving 15 specific rituals. The couple undertake seven steps, rather than exchanging vows, which are performed around a flame in honour of Agni, the god of fire. They literally take one step as they recite each of the following:

'Let us take the first step to provide for our household a nourishing and pure diet, avoiding those foods injurious to healthy living.
'Let us take the second step to develop physical, mental and spiritual powers.
'Let us take the third step to increase our wealth by righteous means and proper use.
'Let us take the fourth step to acquire knowledge, happiness and harmony by mutual love and trust.
'Let us take the fifth step so that we are blessed with strong, virtuous and heroic children.
'Let us take the sixth step for self-restraint and longevity.
'Let us take the seventh step and be true companions and remain lifelong partners by this wedlock.'

A variation of these words makes a lovely addition to any civil ceremony.

Jewish vows

Couples do not traditionally exchange vows and the ceremony structure depends on whether it is Orthodox, Conservative or Reform. But because many couples want to exchange vows, simple wording does form part of the Reform and Conservative ceremonies. For example:

'Do you, ………, take ……… to be your lawfully wedded wife/husband, to love, to honour and to cherish?'

In all ceremonies the marriage vow is sealed when the groom places a ring on his bride's finger and says, 'Behold, you are consecrated to me with this ring according to the laws of Moses and Israel.' Many modern Jewish brides also recite the traditional ring words as they give a ring to their groom.

Muslim vows

Muslim couples do not traditionally exchange vows but listen to the words of the Imam, who talks about the significance of the commitment of marriage and their commitment to Allah. The bride and groom are asked three times if they accept each other in marriage in accordance with the traditional marriage contract. They sign their agreement and the marriage is sealed.

Humanist vows

A humanist marriage ceremony allows complete freedom to say what you like to each other (see page 14), and focuses on the couple's relationship and why they want to make a public declaration to each other. Traditional humanist vows are:

'I acknowledge my love and respect for you and invite you to share my life as I hope to share yours. I promise always to recognise you as an equal and always to be conscious of your development as well as my own. I seek through kindness and understanding to achieve with you the life we have always envisaged.'

'…………, will you have ………… as your wife/husband, to live together in marriage? Will you love her/him, comfort her/him, and honour her/him, in sickness and in health, in sorrow and in joy, as long as you both shall live?'

The vows of marriage

Civil wedding vows

A civil wedding, whether it is performed in a register office or at a building licensed for marriage, is a more relaxed occasion than a religious wedding, but the commitment you are making is just as important.

Once you have booked a date, arrange an appointment with your registrar to discuss the ceremony. Many will have a basic version of the ceremony wording for you to use that you can personalise a little or quite a lot, depending on how strongly you feel about what you want to say. Just remember that this is still a legal undertaking and everything you want to include must reflect the solemnity of the occasion. All wording will need to be agreed in advance with your registrar and you should give them a typed transcript at least two weeks in advance of the big day so that any changes can be made in plenty of time.

Example of a full civil wedding ceremony

(Courtesy of North Yorkshire County Council)

The Wedding Ceremony of (bride) .... and (groom) ....
at (place).. on (date) ....
Music to be played as guests assemble ....
Music to be played as bride enters ....

The Registrar gives a personal introduction to you and your guests.

You may wish to inform the registrar of any guests who have travelled a long distance or any other detail that is worth a mention.

'This place in which we are now met has been duly sanctioned according to law for the celebration of marriages and you are gathered here to witness the joining in matrimony of ………. and ………. If there is any person here who knows of any lawful impediment to this marriage, they should declare it now.'

A reading could be included here.

Title of reading ....
Author ....
Read by ....

'Before you are joined in matrimony I have to remind you of the solemn and binding character of the vows you are about to make. Marriage according to the law of this country is the union of one man with one woman voluntarily entered into for life to the exclusion of all others.

'Now I am going to ask each of you in turn to declare that you do not know of any lawful reason why you should not be married to each other. Please repeat after me:

The vows of marriage

'"I do solemnly declare that I know not of any lawful impediment why I, ... may not be joined in matrimony to ...."

'The purpose of marriage is that you may always love, care for and support each other through all the joys and sorrows of life; and that love may be fulfilled in a relationship of permanent and continuing commitment. We trust that these things may come true of you both.'

And/or

'......... and .... wish to marry, for in each other's company they have found fulfilment and love. As a consequence of this love they have drawn closer to each other and now wish to affirm publicly their relationship and to offer each other the security that comes from vows sincerely made and faithfully kept.

'(The Institution of) Marriage must be entered into freely, voluntarily and with the full and unreserved consent of you both. Therefore:

'Do you, ..., take .... here present to be your lawful wedded wife? (Groom to respond).

'Do you, ..., take .... here present to be your lawful wedded husband? (Bride to respond).

'Now the solemn moment has come for these two persons to make the contract of marriage before you, their witnesses, will you all please stand. Please repeat after me:

'"I call upon these persons here present to witness that I .... do take thee .... to be my lawful wedded wife (or husband)."'

Below are optional vows, which may be included in your civil ceremony and read or repeated by the bride and groom.

'I promise to love and care for you and be faithful to you always. May we look to our future together with hope, happiness and joy and remembering this day never allow anything to destroy the feeling that we share for each other.'

Or:
'I promise to love you tenderly, to cherish and respect you; to laugh with you and cry with you; to nourish you with my gentleness and comfort you with my strength; to walk with you in sorrow, joy, illness and age; facing life together, wherever it may take us.'

Or:
'I, ..., acknowledge my love and respect for you and invite you to share my life as I hope to share yours. May we look to our future together with hope, happiness and joy. I shall seek through kindness and understanding to achieve with you the life we have envisaged.'

'We now come to the giving of the wedding ring(s). This is the traditional and ancient way of sealing the contract you have made and is the outward sign of the lifelong promises you have made to each other. ...., place the ring on ....'s finger, and repeat after me:

'"I give you this ring as a symbol of my endless love for you. All that I am and all that I have I bring to you. May this ring remind us of this moment and the commitment I have made to you."'

If only one ring is to be given: 'I accept this ring' (then as above).

A reading could be included here:
Title of reading ....
Author ....
Read by ....

The vows of marriage

'You have both made the declaration prescribed by law and you have made a solemn and binding contract with each other in the presence of your witnesses, family and friends here this morning/afternoon. It is my privilege and pleasure to tell you that you are now husband and wife. Congratulations.'

Signing of the register
A musical interlude could be included here:

Music ....

Your guests will have the chance to take photographs of you after the signing of the register, if you wish. Music to be played as bride and groom exit.

Writing your own wedding vows
There is nothing to say you cannot put together your own order of service for a civil ceremony. Ask your registrar for an outline of what legally must be included and some sample wording; you can then add your vows and readings around this.

To bring a more personal flavour to your wedding vows, start by asking yourselves a few key questions before committing pen to paper:

- Why are you getting married?
- What does marriage mean to each of you?
- What will it take to make your marriage work?
- What do you love about your partner?
- Which qualities do you most admire about him/her?
- What are your similarities? What are your differences?
- What do you want to achieve in the future?
- What do you want to say in front of your families and friends about your relationship and future together?
- Are there any appropriate words – from a song or poem – that say something special about your relationship that could be included?

You can work on your vows separately or together, whatever suits you best. You can recite exactly the same vows to each other, or say something individual. Just bear in mind that personalised vows want to be heartfelt (without being overly gushing) and should say something meaningful about your relationship, your hopes for the future and your commitment to a lifelong marriage. It is best to keep anything too flippant or intimate for a private moment between the two of you.

You can find inspiration for what to say from many sources. I hope that you find this book is a great starting point, but also feel free to borrow words and phrases that appeal to you from religious texts, favourite songs, prose, poems and quotes. This is one time in your life when it is considered okay to be inspired by the words of others. It is also acceptable to tailor someone else's words to make them more appropriate to you. The website www.youandyourwedding.co.uk has an excellent section on vows and readings to help you get started.

If the text is particularly old, you might want to subtly update it: for example to change 'man and wife' to 'husband and wife' for a sense of equality. If you are using just part of a larger body of work, make sure that the part you choose is appropriate. Many a poet has waxed lyrical about love – and using just a few lines out of context may seem okay, until you discover the object of his desire is dead! Lesson learned: read the whole work and make sure you understand the meaning.

When in doubt...
Inspirational phrases to help with writer's block:

- For as long as we both shall live.
- From this day forward.
- I promise with all my heart.
- From the bottom of my heart.
- I give myself to you.
- My partner in life.
- All that I am, I give to you.
- You are my one true love, above all others.
- I will always be by your side.
- This is my solemn vow to you.
- I will share my life with you.

The vows of marriage

Start writing your vows by making notes, jotting down key words and phrases that express what you feel. Begin with how you feel about your partner and how good you are together, then move on to what you hope to achieve in the future. It is meant to sound personal, so include your partner's name and make references to your lives rather than using phrases that are too broad and could apply to anyone; but don't make references too obscure, because you want your audience to understand them, too. Keep phrases positive and avoid negative language. A little light humour is ok, but err on the side of caution. Even a simple civil ceremony is a solemn occasion and riotous laughter is not appropriate.

Write from the heart and don't be afraid of sounding a little soppy; it's your wedding day, after all. When it comes to length, keep it short and sweet. Your vows are the most important part of the ceremony but they shouldn't be long-winded. Anything longer than about a minute of spoken text (that's 200–250 words) is probably too long.

Once you have a list of favourite words you can start to put them into context within the framework of your order of service.

Sample wedding vows – a beginning

'I, ………, choose you, ………, as my best friend for life's great journey.'
'I, ………, choose you, ………, to embark on the journey of marriage with me.'
'I, ……… , take you, ………, as my soul mate and lifelong companion.'
'I, ……… , take you, ……… , to be my wife, my friend, my lover, my confidante.'

Sample wedding vows – the middle

'Together, we can accomplish anything.'
'Together, we will be stronger than we could ever be alone.'
'Together, we will share our love with the world.'
'Together, our love will grow into a bond too strong to break.'
'Through the good and the bad, I want you by my side.'

Sample wedding vows – declarations

'In sickness, I will nurse you back to health. In health, I will encourage you on your chosen road. In sadness, I will help you to remember the good times. In happiness, I will make precious memories with you. In poverty, I will do all that I can to make our love rich. And in wealth, I will never let our love grow poor.'

'When you need someone to encourage you, I want it to be me. When you need a helping hand, I want it to be mine. When you long for someone to smile at, turn to me. When you have something to share, share it with me.'

'Though life may not always be as perfect as it is at this moment, I vow always to keep my love as pure as it is today. I promise to be there for you through laughter and tears, in sickness and health, for richer and for poorer. I promise to be there for you for all your life, whatever life may bring.'

'I promise to keep the good memories alive, and to let the bad ones die. I vow not to let the sun go down on our anger and to treat each morning as a new day to love you. I will not forsake you or these vows that we have made, but strive to show you my love for the rest of our lives. This is my promise to you, today and forever.'

Putting it all together: some examples

'From this moment, I, ………, take you, ………, as my wife, my best friend and my partner for life. I pledge to honour, encourage and support you through our journey together. When the path becomes difficult, I promise to stand by you so that together we can accomplish more than we ever could alone. Every day I promise to work at our love and always make you a priority in my life. With every beat of my heart, I will love you. This is my solemn vow.'

'I, ………, take you, ………, as my best friend for life. I am so in love with you that I want to promise to stand beside you through thick and thin, through good times and bad, through joy and sorrow. I want to spend the rest of my life hearing your thoughts and seeing your dreams. I promise to do my best to make our lives better and better from this day forward. This is my solemn vow.'

The vows of marriage

'We are here today in front of our families and friends to make a lasting commitment to one another. I want the world to know that you bring joy to my life. I affirm the special bond between us and promise that from this day onwards I will be your confidante, your best friend and will share all your hopes and dreams. In recognition of this, I, …………, take you, …………, to be my husband. With this vow I promise to be a loyal and trustworthy wife and to love you whatever the circumstances.'

Words of love

If you find yourself stuck for what to say, be inspired by this list to see what applies to your partner and the way you feel about one another:

	Faithful	Partner
	Forever	Promise
	Friendship	Share
	Future	Soul mate
	Goals	Strength
	Growth	Togetherness
Adore	Happiness	True
Adventure	Honest	Trust
Aspirations	Hope	Understanding
Beginning	Inspiration	Unity
Blessed	Journey	Values
Bond	Joy	Wishes
Challenges	Learning	
Comfort	Loyalty	
Committed	Nurture	
Complement		
Complete		
Devoted		
Enduring		

Once you are both happy with what you want to say, practise reading it out loud. Sometimes what reads well in your head doesn't sound quite right when you say it, and the odd phrase may need to be revised so that the sentences flow and you feel comfortable saying them. Ask a trusted friend to give you an honest opinion.

Give a typed copy of all your proposed text – including the words for all songs and readings – to your registrar to check that it all meets with his or her requirements. Submit this at least two weeks in advance to give you enough time for amendments.

Delivering your vows

You will no doubt have read and re-read your vows many times before the wedding day and familiarised yourself with the words. If you think you can commit everything to memory, great. Just don't underestimate how nervous you may be feeling, because that is when your mind might go blank!

As a safeguard, write out your vows on a cue card or give a copy of the words to the officiant, chief bridesmaid or best man to hold until the big moment arrives. You might not need it, but you could be very glad to have it close at hand.

You will turn to face one another as you say your vows and it is quite likely that you will feel very emotional, perhaps starting to cry as you listen to what's being said or as you start to speak yourself. Don't worry about a few tears; everyone will love you even more for it. Just take a moment to compose yourself and then carry on. You only get to say your vows once, so speak slowly and savour every word.

Renewal of wedding vows

At some point in the future, after (it is hoped) many happy years of marriage, you may want to consider renewing your marriage vows to celebrate your relationship and your life together so far. Many couples exchange the same vows as at their original ceremony, but it is also your chance to pledge your commitment for the years ahead, as well as saying something about the love you have for those important to you. For example:

The vows of marriage

'My darling, ……….., it was 30 years ago that we first pledged our commitment to one another, but it seems like just yesterday that I was standing across from my beautiful bride. You have been my rock through good times and bad. We have experienced so much together – laughter and tears, joy and sorrow – and I have loved you every step of the way. You have given me our wonderful children ……… and ………, and for that I can never thank you enough.

'Today, I want to renew our marriage vows and again promise my love and my life to you. Whatever the years to come may bring, I promise to be there for you in sickness and in health. I am here to be your supporter, your confidant and always your best friend. I have been blessed with you by my side for the last 30 years and look forward to spending the rest of my life with you. I love you.'

Thoughtful touches
Sweet ideas to make any ceremony even more memorable:

- Borrow a tradition from the USA and light unity candles to symbolise the joining together of two families.
- Sprinkle the aisle with lavender heads – these will release an amazing fragrance as the bridal party come into the venue.
- Print a picture of the bride and groom as babies on the cover of the order of service or use a grandparents' wedding photograph.
- Offer each guest a pack of tissues along with the order of service.
- Have your order of service printed on fan-shaped cards – very welcome in high summer during a lengthy religious ceremony.
- Forget bride's family on the left, groom's on the right – ask friends and family to mingle.
- Give the congregation mini bottles of bubbles to use instead of confetti.
- Release a pair of doves as you leave the venue as man and wife.
- Organise for church bells to peal in celebration of your marriage.

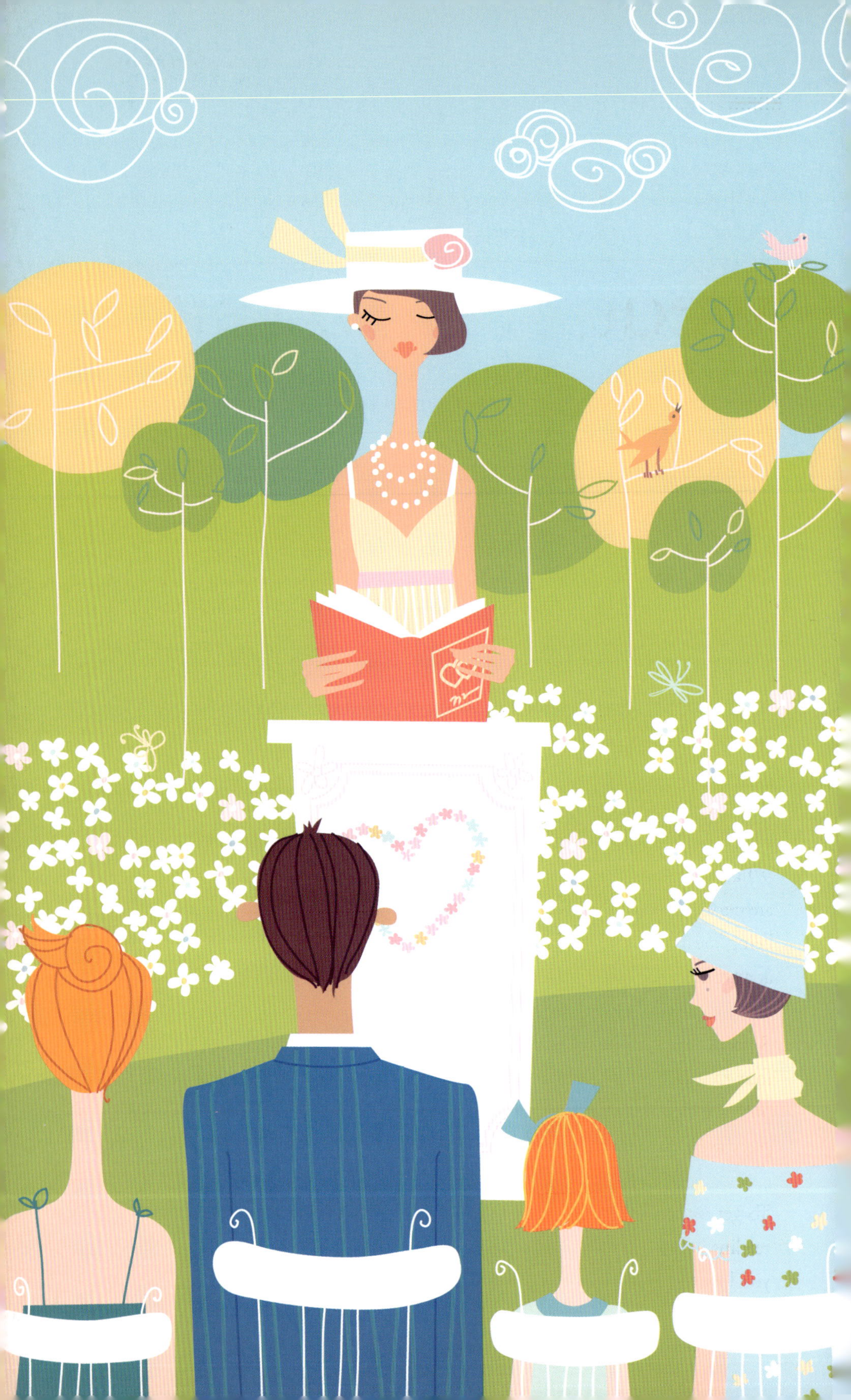

Chapter 3

All about wedding readings

A selection of carefully chosen and well-presented readings is an important part of any wedding ceremony. But where are the best places to find inspiration, and who do you choose to put into the spotlight?

Writers throughout history have waxed lyrical about all manner of subjects suitable to include as part of your wedding: words on love, family, relationships, marriage, friends, children and the future. So look to literature throughout the ages to find a poem, sonnet or piece of prose that appeals to you.

What is important as you begin your research is to make sure you find words that are personal to you and your groom – something that your guests will recognise as being meaningful to you – rather than just a generic reading that could be heard at anyone's wedding.

Readings can be short but it's unusual for them to be lengthy – between two and four minutes' duration is about right. There is no need to read a whole poem if only a select number of verses are appropriate. The reader simply introduces the piece as 'an extract from the work of…' inserting the name and the writer.

To get a feeling for whether the reading sounds right and works for timing, try reading the pieces aloud. It's very misleading if you only read the text silently, as you lose the impact of a spoken piece.

What will you choose?

If you are having a religious ceremony you will be bound by traditional readings from the Bible. Your vicar or priest will be able to give you examples of these, but there will still be lots of choice. Some ministers will be happy for you to include a suitable work of classical literature – Shakespeare, for example – but you will need to ask permission first, as some will prefer that you stick to the Scriptures.

To find inspiration for a civil ceremony, look to your past. Do you have an affinity with a particular poet, perhaps someone you studied at university that evokes memories? Have you ever watched a performance of *Romeo and Juliet* together? Is there a modern poet's work that attracts you? Do you have a favourite song? The lyrics are, after all, just words set to music.

You can also look to your cultural background for ideas. Do either of you have Scottish, Welsh or Irish ancestry that you could mention? Or perhaps you have some ethnic blood that means you can borrow from a Hindu or Buddhist ceremony.

If the words are about beauty or perhaps the bride, it's usual to get a man to read them. If the reading is about the attributes of a man, then it's more appropriate for a woman to read them.

Honour a deceased relative or friend by dedicating a reading to them.

If you find several short readings that you like, you can ask several people to read them, introducing themselves by announcing, 'Some thoughts on the wonderful institution of marriage…' or 'Where would we be without love…?'.

Of course, there is nothing to say that you cannot write something especially for the occasion yourselves. Now that would be really personal!

Whatever you choose, it is usual to print the words of the readings in your order of service, with proper credits to the author and the source, so that your guests can follow what is being said. If the readings are personal, you may like to have them printed and presented to each guest as a favour to take home as a memento.

All about wedding readings

Who will give the reading?

Asking someone to do a reading is a great opportunity to involve close family or friends who are not part of the main bridal party. There is nothing to say that parents and grandparents cannot make a reading, and even the bride and groom have been known to stand up and read something that is particularly meaningful to them – you can choose whatever feels right for your day.

What is important is that the readers have the confidence to speak in public. They need to be people who are unlikely to be overcome with nerves, either mumbling their way through or, worse still, refusing to perform at the last minute. Whoever you ask, give them plenty of notice and don't be offended if they refuse. Not everyone enjoys being in the spotlight.

The readers can be involved in the choice of reading – they might have a favourite passage that fits the bill perfectly – or you can ask them to read your chosen texts. They need to practise several times in the weeks leading up to the wedding, ideally in a large room with someone who will give an honest opinion of how it sounds. Most people tend to speak too quickly when they are nervous and often forget to breathe, so it all comes out in a bit of a rush. If you are having a wedding rehearsal, this is the ideal opportunity for the speakers to become comfortable with the venue.

Most readers will be happiest to have their words written out on a piece of paper, but the more they practise the more likely it will be that they can, at least occasionally, look up and address their audience. Relying purely on memory probably isn't a good idea, because even the most confident person can be struck by an attack of nerves and forget what they are supposed to say.

Some people find that they like to highlight text, or colour-code the print to make it easier to glance at their text now and then while they are giving the reading.

Making readings part of the ceremony

Depending on the formality of the wedding, it is usual to include between one and three readings in the order of service. Speak to your officiant about the most suitable points for their inclusion, probably after the first hymn or the welcome address, before the signing of the register and just before the recessional. The tone of the reading can then be tailored to suit the moment; for example, a reading about love and friendship is a nice place to start and something about new beginnings a good way to end the ceremony.

The reader is usually introduced by the officiant and makes his or her way up to the front of the room, either to the altar or to stand to one side of the bride and groom at a civil ceremony. At an intimate civil wedding with fewer guests, the reader can probably just stand up and speak, rather than coming to the front of the room, to add to the relaxed atmosphere.

Larger venues may have a microphone available, in which case the reader should definitely have practised with this beforehand. It can take a moment to get the pitch of the voice just right and there's nothing worse than shocking the audience with a booming voice or a screeching microphone in the hands of a novice!

Inspiration for readings

There is a comprehensive selection of favourite readings for religious and civil weddings in the following two chapters (pages 38–127). You will also find more ideas on website www.youandyourwedding.co.uk in Vows and Readings.

The following websites and reference books should also prove useful as you begin your search for the right words.

Websites for religious ceremonies

www.baptist.org.uk .... *The Baptist Church*
www.biblegateway.com .... *Service for researching and reading Scriptures online*
www.catholic-ew.org.uk .... *The Catholic Church in England and Wales*
www.chbookshop.co.uk .... *Church of England online bookshop*
www.churchofscotland.org.uk .... *The Church of Scotland*

All about wedding readings

www.cofe.anglican.org/lifeevents/weddings .... *The Church of England*
www.jmc-uk.org .... *The Jewish Marriage Council*
www.methodist.org.uk .... *The Methodist Church*

Websites for civil ceremonies

www.groni.gov.uk .... *General Register Office for Northern Ireland*
www.gro-scotland.gov.uk .... *General Register Office for Scotland*
www.ons.gov.uk .... *General Register Office for England and Wales*

Websites for poetry and prose

www.biography.com .... *Useful for background details on anyone you are quoting*
www.everypoet.com .... *Comprehensive site for searching for poems*
www.plagiarist.com .... *Links to poems and poets*
www.poetryarchive.org .... *Website aiming to make poetry accessible to all*
www.poetry-online.org .... *Themed resource providing works by popular poets*

Reference books for poetry and readings

Wedding Readings & Musical Ideas, Rev John Wynburne & Alison Gibbs, Foulsham, ISBN 978-0-572-02861-9

The Big Book of Wedding Readings, Confetti.co.uk, Conran Octopus Ltd, ISBN 978-1-840-91481-8

The New Faber Book of Love Poems, James Fenton, Faber and Faber, ISBN 978-0-571-21814-1

The Nation's Favourite Love Poems, Daisy Goodwin, BBC Books, ISBN 978-0-563-38378-9

Love Letters in the Sand: The Love Poems of Khalil Gibran, Khalil Gibran, Souvenir Press Ltd, ISBN 978-0-285-63721-4

The Penguin Book of the Sonnet: 500 Years of a Classic Tradition in English, Phillis Levin, Penguin Books Ltd, ISBN 978-0-140-58929-0

The Oxford Treasury of Classic Poems, Michael Harrison and Christopher Stuart-Clark, Oxford University Press, ISBN 978-0-192-76289-4

The Creative Jewish Wedding Book, Gabrielle Kaplan-Mayer, Jewish Lights Publishing, ISBN 978-1-580-23194-7

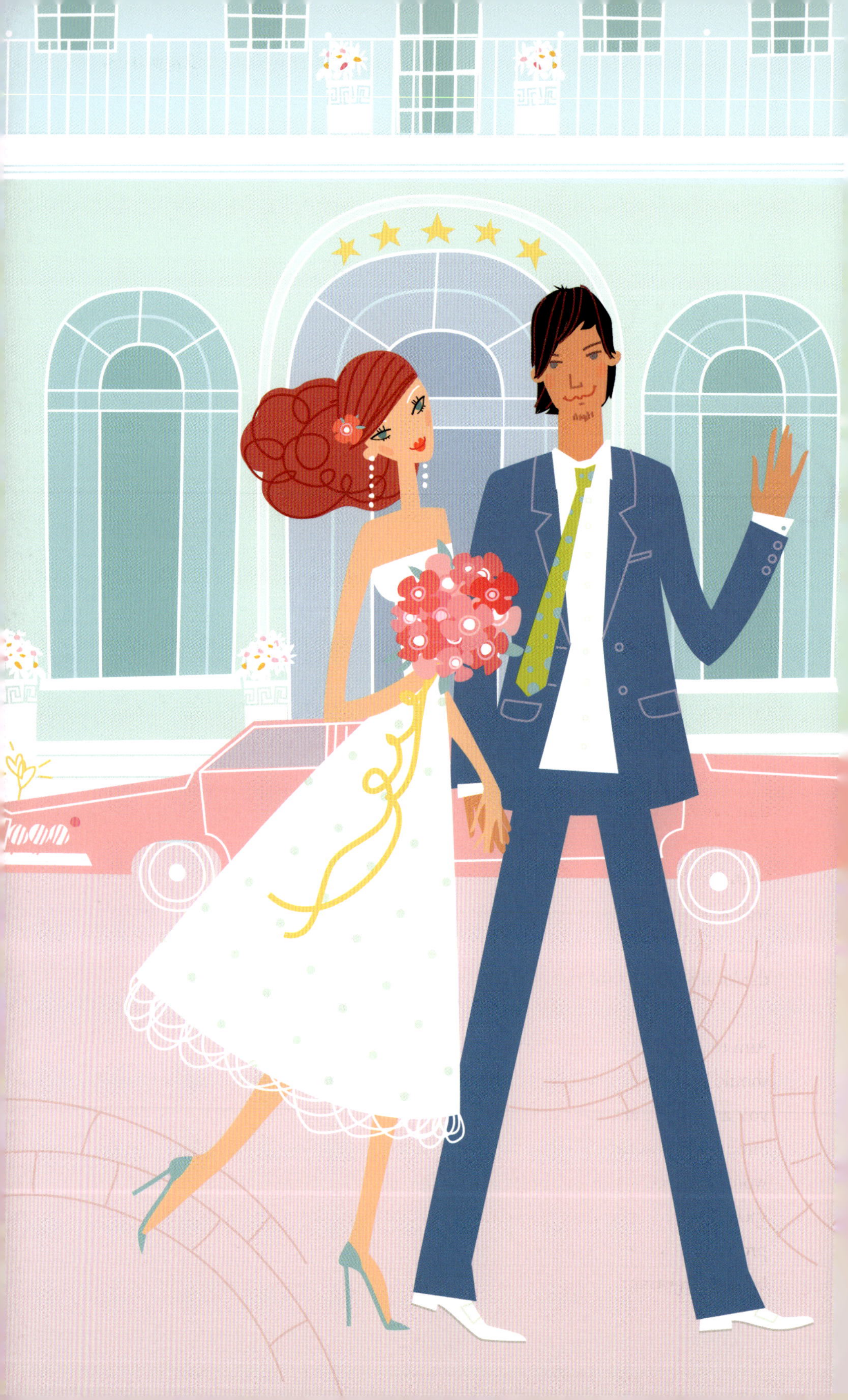

Chapter 4

Readings for a civil ceremony

The civil marriage ceremony allows you the freedom to express your emotions, and there is a wealth of words out there to help you tell the world what you are feeling as you become husband and wife.

A civil ceremony, whether it is held in a register office or in a building approved for marriage, is more straightforward than a traditional religious ceremony, but you still want it to feel like the momentous occasion it is. Legally, a civil wedding can be very brief, but having gathered together friends and family, you might want to think about putting together an order of service that feels like a celebration.

Spend a few hours in the library looking through books on love and marriage as well as on the internet – the website www.youandyourwedding.co.uk is a good place to start. Your registrar will also be happy to offer some suggestions. Many of the local authority websites have readings within the marriage section, as well.

Aim to include at least one reading that you like or that is meaningful to you. You should be looking for a poem or piece of prose that expresses something about how you are feeling and the big commitment you are making to one another. At the same time, you can also have a go at writing your own wedding vows, the actual words that you say as you become husband and wife (see pages 25–30). Nothing spoken or sung at a civil ceremony can have any religious connotations and all your proposed vows, readings and musical choices will need to be approved beforehand by your registrar.

Popular readings for a civil wedding

On your wedding day

Today is a day you will always remember,
The greatest in anyone's life;
You'll start off the day just two people in love,
And end it as husband and wife.

It's a brand new beginning, the start of a journey,
With moments to cherish and treasure;
And although there'll be times when you both disagree,
These will surely be outweighed by pleasure.

You'll have heard many words of advice in the past,
When the secrets of marriage were spoken;
But you know that the answers lie hidden inside,
Where the bond of true love lies unbroken.

So live happy forever as lovers and friends,
It's the dawn of a new life for you,
As you stand there together with love in your eyes,
From the moment you whisper 'I do'.

And with luck all your hopes and your dreams can be real,
May success find its way to your hearts;
Tomorrow can bring you the greatest of joys,
But today is the day it all starts.

Anon

Sonnet LXIX

Maybe nothingness is to be without your presence,
Without you moving, slicing the noon
Like a blue flower, without you walking
Later through the fog and the cobbles,
Without the light you carry in your hand,
Golden, which maybe others will not see,
Which maybe no one knew was growing
Like the red beginnings of a rose.

In short, without your presence: without your coming
Suddenly, incitingly, to know my life,
Gust of a rosebush, wheat of wind:
Since then I am because you are,
Since then you are, I am, we are,
And through love I will be, you will be, we'll be.

Pablo Neruda

You can give without loving
You can give without loving but you can never love without giving.

The great acts of love are done by those who are habitually performing small acts of kindness. We pardon to the extent that we love. Love is knowing that even when you are alone, you will never be truly alone again. And great happiness of life is the conviction that we are loved. Loved for ourselves. And even loved in spite of ourselves.
Victor Hugo, from Les Miserables

The beauty of love

The question is asked: 'Is there anything more beautiful in life than a young couple clasping hands and pure hearts in the path of marriage? Can there be anything more beautiful than young love?' And the answer is given: 'Yes, there is a more beautiful thing. It is the spectacle of an old man and an old woman finishing their journey together on that path. Their hands are gnarled but still clasped; their faces are seamed but still radiant; their hearts are physically bowed and tired but still strong with love and devotion. Yes, there is a more beautiful thing than young love. Old love.'

Anon

Tribal wish of the Iroquois

May you have a safe tent
And no sorrow as you travel.
May happiness attend you in all your paths.
May you keep a heart like the morning.
And may you come slow to the four corners.
Where man says goodnight.

Anon

Extract from a Native American wedding ceremony

May the sun bring you new happiness by day;
May the moon softly restore you by night;
May the rain wash away your worries
And the breeze blow new strength into your being.
And all the days of your life
May you walk gently through the world and know its beauty.

Anon

Apache marriage blessing

Now you will feel no rain, for each of you will be the shelter for each other. Now you will feel no cold, for each of you will be the warmth for the other. Now you are two persons, but there is only one life before. Go now to your dwelling place to enter into the days of your life together. And may your days be good and long upon the earth.

Treat yourselves and each other with respect, and remind yourselves often of what brought you together. Give the highest priority to the tenderness, gentleness and kindness that your connection deserves. When frustration, difficulty and fear assail your relationship – as they threaten all relationships at one time or another – remember to focus on what is right between you, not only the part which seems wrong. In this way, you can ride out the storms when clouds hide the face of the sun in your lives – remembering that even if you lose sight of it for a moment, the sun is still there. And if each of you takes responsibility for the quality of your life together, it will be marked by abundance and delight.

Anon

To my bride

To my bride, I give you my heart
Sharing love each day, from the very start.
To my bride, I give you my kiss
Filling each day with joy and bliss.
To my bride I give you my being
To love, to play, to work and to sing
To my bride I give you my mind
Learning each day to be more kind.
To my bride I give you my soul
Growing together to be more whole.
To my bride I give you my life
Rejoicing each day that you are my wife.
Steven Reiser

You are my husband

You are my husband
You are my wife
My feet shall run because of you
My feet dance because of you
My heart shall beat because of you
My eyes see because of you
My mind thinks because of you
And I shall love because of you.
Eskimo Love Song

Readings for a civil ceremony

Marriage

The die is cast, come weal, come woe,
Two lives are joined together,
For better or for worse, the link
Which naught but death can sever.
The die is cast, come grief, come joy,
Come richer, or come poorer,
If love but binds the mystic tie,
Blest is the bridal hour.

Mary Weston Fordham

Our great adventure

We are today still dizzy with the astonishment of love.
We are surrounded by affection – by smiles and kindliness,
By flowers and music and gifts and celebration.
Yet they enclose a silence
Where we are close with one another.
My eyes see only you.
I hear nothing but the words
We speak to one another
This is the day we start our life together.
This is our new beginning.

Pamela Dugdale

A dedication to my wife

To whom I owe the leaping delight
That quicken my senses in our waking time
And the rhythm that governs the repose
Of our sleeping time
The breathing in unison
Of lovers whose bodies smell of each other.
Who think the same thoughts
Without the need of speech
And babble the same speech
Without need of meaning
No peevish winter wind
Shall chill
No sullen wither
The roses in the rose garden which
Is ours and ours only
But this dedication is for others to read:
These are my private words
Addressed to you in public.
T S Eliot

A Chinese poem

I want to be your friend forever and ever
When the hills are all flat and the rivers run dry
When the trees blossom in winter
And the snow falls in summer,
When heaven and earth mix –
Not till then will I part from you.

Anon

Readings for a civil ceremony

Today I married my best friend

Today I married my best friend,
Our bond complete, it hath no end,
We share one soul, we share one heart,
A perfect time – a perfect start.

With these rings we share together,
Love so close to last forever,
This special day – two special hearts,
Let nothing keep this love apart.

Rachel Elizabeth Cooper

This day I married my best friend

This day I married my best friend
… the one I laugh with as we share life's wondrous zest,
as we find new enjoyments and experience all that's best.
… the one I live for because the world seems brighter
as our happy times are better and our burdens feel much lighter.
… the one I love with every fibre of my soul.
We used to feel vaguely incomplete, now together we are whole.

Anon

Married love

You and I
Have so much love
That it burns like a fire
In which we bake a lump of clay
Moulded into a figure of you
And a figure of me
Then we take both of them
And break them into pieces
And mix the pieces with water
And mould again a figure of you
And a figure of me
I am in your clay
You are in my clay
In life we share a single quilt
In death we will share one coffin.

Kuan Tao-Sheng

A marriage

You are holding up a ceiling
with both arms. It is very heavy,
but you must hold it up, or else
it will fall down on you. Your arms
are tired, terribly tired,
and, as the day goes on, it feels
as if either your arms or the ceiling
will soon collapse.

But then,
unexpectedly,
something wonderful happens:
Someone,
a man or a woman,
walks into the room
and holds their arms up
to the ceiling beside you.

So you finally get
to take down your arms.
You feel the relief of respite,
the blood flowing back
to your fingers and arms.
And when your partner's arms tire,
you hold up your own
to relieve him again.
And it can go on like this
for many years
without the house falling.

Michael Blumenthal

True love

True love is a sacred flame
That burns eternally,
And none can dim its special glow
Or change its destiny.
True love speaks in tender tones
And hears with gentle ear,
True love gives with open heart
And true love conquers fear.
True love makes no harsh demands,
It neither rules nor binds,
And true love holds with gentle hands
The hearts that it entwines.

Anon

Wedding day

Now comes the knitting, the tying, the entwining into one,
Mysterious involvement of two, whole separate people
Into something altogether strange and changing and lovely.
Nothing can ever be, we will never be the same again;
Not merged into each other irrevocably but rather
From now on we go the same way, in the same direction,
Agreeing not to leave each other lonely, or discouraged or behind,
I will do my best to keep my promises to you and keep you warm;
And we will make our wide bed beneath the bright and ragged quilt
Of all the yesterdays that make us who we are,
The strengths and frailties we bring to this marriage,
And we will be rich indeed.

Anon

These I can promise

I cannot promise you a life of sunshine;
I cannot promise riches, wealth, or gold;
I cannot promise you an easy pathway

That leads away from change or growing old.

But I can promise all my heart's devotion;
A smile to chase away your tears of sorrow;
A love that's ever true and ever growing;
A hand to hold in yours through each tomorrow.
Yes, I'll marry you.

Anon

Foundations of marriage

Love, trust, and forgiveness are the foundations of marriage. In marriage, many days will bring happiness, while other days may be sad. But together, two hearts can overcome everything... In marriage, all of the moments won't be exciting or romantic, and sometimes worries and anxiety will be overwhelming. But together, two hearts that accept will find comfort together. Recollections of past joys, pains, and shared feelings will be the glue that holds everything together during even the worst and most insecure moments. Reaching out to each other as a friend, and becoming the confidant and companion that the other one needs, is the true magic and beauty of any two people together. It's inspiring in each other a dream or a feeling, and having faith in each other and not giving up... even when all the odds say to quit. It's allowing each other to be vulnerable, to be himself or herself, even when the opinions or thoughts aren't in total agreement or exactly what you'd like them to be. It's getting involved and showing interest in each other, really listening and being available, the way any best friend should be. Exactly three things need to be remembered in a marriage if it is to be a mutual bond of sharing, caring, and loving throughout life: love, trust, and forgiveness.

Regina Hill

Never marry but for love

Never marry but for love; but see that thou lovest what is lovely. If love be not the chief motive, thou wilt soon grow weary of a married state and stray from thy promise, to search out thy pleasures in forbidden places...

Between a man and his wife nothing ought to rule but love ... As love ought to bring them together, so it is the best way to keep them well together.

A husband and wife that love and value one another show their children... that they should do so too. Others visibly lose authority in their families by their contempt of one another, and teach their children to be unnatural by their own examples.

Let not enjoyment lessen, but augment, affection; it being the basest of passions to like when we have not, what we slight when we possess.

Here it is we ought to search out our pleasure, where the field is large and full of variety, and of an enduring nature; sickness, poverty or disgrace being not able to shake it because it is not under the moving influences of worldly contingencies.

Nothing can be more entire and without reserve; nothing more zealous, affectionate and sincere; nothing more contented than such a couple, nor greater temporal felicity than to be one of them.

William Penn

I promise

I promise to give you the best of myself
and to ask of you no more than you can give.
I promise to respect you as your own person
and to realise that your interests, desires and needs
are no less important than my own.
I promise to share with you my time and my attention
and to bring joy, strength and imagination to our relationship.

I promise to keep myself open to you,
to let you see through the window of my world into
my innermost fears
and feelings, secrets and dreams.
I promise to grow along with you,
to be willing to face changes in order to keep our
relationship alive and exciting.
I promise to love you in good times and in bad,
with all I have to give and all I feel inside in the only
way I know how.
Completely and forever.

Dorothy R Colgan

Hand of the bride and groom

(Bride's name), please face (groom's name) and hold his hands, palms up, so you may see the gift that they are to you. These are the hands that will passionately love you and cherish you through the years, for a lifetime of happiness. These are the hands that will countless times wipe the tears from your eyes: tears of sorrow and tears of joy. These are the hands that will comfort you in illness, and hold you when fear or grief fill you. These are the hands that will give you support and celebrate with you in your accomplishments.

(Groom's name), please hold (bride's name)'s hands, palms up, where you may see the gift that they are to you. These are the hands that will hold you tight as you struggle through difficult times. They are the hands that will comfort you when you are sick or console you when you are grieving. These are the hands that will passionately love you and cherish you through the years, for a lifetime of happiness. These are the hands that will give you support as she encourages you to fulfil your dreams. Together, as a team, everything you wish for can be realised.

Anon

Readings for a civil ceremony

Dove poem

Two doves meeting in the sky
Two loves hand in hand eye to eye
Two parts of a loving whole
Two hearts and a single soul.
Two stars shining big and bright
Two fires bringing warmth and light
Two songs played in perfect tune
Two flowers growing into bloom.
Two doves gliding in the air
Two loves free without a care
Two parts of a loving whole
Two hearts and a single soul.

Anon

I knew that I had been touched by love

I knew that I had been touched by love the first time I saw you and I felt your warmth, and I heard your laughter.

I knew that I had been touched by love when I was hurting from something that happened, and you came along and made the hurt go away.

I knew that I had been touched by love when I stopped making plans with my friends and started dreaming dreams with you.

I knew that I had been touched by love when I suddenly stopped thinking in terms of 'me' and started thinking in terms of 'we'.

I knew that I had been touched by love when suddenly I couldn't make decisions by myself any more.

I knew that I had been touched by love the first time we spent alone together, and I knew that I wanted to stay with you forever because I had never felt this touched by love.

Anon

Readings for a civil ceremony

A red, red rose

My love is like a red red rose
That's newly sprung in June
My love is like the melody
That's sweetly played in tune.

As fair as thou art, my bonnie lass
So deep in love am I
And I will love thee still, my dear,
Till a' the seas gang dry.
Till a' the seas gang dry, my dear
And the rocks melt with the sun.
I will love thee still, my dear
While the sands o' life shall run.

And fare thee well, my only love!
And fare thee well a while
And I will come again my love,
Though it were ten thousand miles.
Robert Burns

The depth of love

Real love is all-consuming, desperate yearning for the beloved, who is perceived as different, mysterious, and elusive. The depth of love is measured by the intensity of obsession with the loved one. There is little time or attention for other interests or pursuits, because so much energy is focused on recalling past encounters or imagining future ones. Often, great obstacles must be overcome, and thus there is an element of suffering in true love. Another indication of the depth of love is the willingness to endure pain and hardship for the sake of the relationship. Associated with real love are feelings of excitement, rapture, drama, anxiety, tension, mystery and yearning.

Real love is a partnership to which two caring people are deeply committed. These people share many basic values, interests and goals, and tolerate good-naturedly their individual differences. The depth of love is measured by the mutual trust and respect they feel toward each other. Their relationship allows each to be more fully expressive, creative, and productive in the world. There is much joy in shared experiences both past and present, as well as those that are anticipated. Each views the other as his/her dearest and most cherished friend. Another measure of the depth of love is the willingness to look honestly at oneself in order to promote the growth of the relationship and the deepening of intimacy. Associated with real love are feelings of serenity, devotion, understanding, companionship, mutual support, and comfort.

Robin Norwood, from Women Who Love Too Much

Readings for a civil ceremony

First love

I ne'er was struck before that hour
With love so sudden and so sweet
Her face it bloomed like a sweet flower
And stole my heart away complete
My face turned a deadly pale
My legs refused to walk away
And when she looked what could I ail
My life and all seemed turned to clay.

And then my blood rushed to my face
And took my eyesight quite away
The trees and bushes round the place
Seemed midnight at noon day
I could not see a single thing
Words from my eyes did start
They spoke as chords do from the string
And blood burned round my heart.

Are flowers the winter's choice
Is love's bed always snow?
She seemed to hear my silent voice
Not love's appeals to know
I never saw so sweet a face
As that I stood before
My heart has left its dwelling place
And can return no more.

John Clare

A good wedding cake

4lbs of love
½lb of good looks
1lb of sweet temper
1lb of butter of youth
1lb of blindness of fault
1lb of pounded wit
1lb of good humour
2 tablespoons of sweet argument
1 pint of rippling laughter
1 wine glass of common sense
Dash of modesty

Put the love, good looks and sweet temper into a well-furnished house. Beat the butter of youth to a cream, and mix well together with the blindness of faults. Stir the pounded wit and good humour into the sweet argument, then add the rippling laughter and common sense. Add a dash of modesty and work the whole together until everything is well mixed. Bake gently forever.

Anon

I will be here

If in the morning when you wake,
If the sun does not appear,
I will be here.
If in the dark we lose sight of love,
Hold my hand and have no fear,
I will be here.

I will be here,
When you feel like being quiet,
When you need to speak your mind I will listen.
Through the winning, losing, and trying we'll be together,
And I will be here.
If in the morning when you wake,
If the future is unclear,
I will be here.
As sure as seasons were made for change,
Our lifetimes were made for years,
I will be here.

I will be here,
And you can cry on my shoulder,
When the mirror tells us we're older.
I will hold you, to watch you grow in beauty,
And tell you all the things you are to me.
We'll be together and I will be here.
I will be true to the promises I've made,
To you and to the one who gave you to me.
I will be here.

Stephen Chapman Curtis

The colour of my love

I'll paint a sun to warm your heart
Knowing that we'll never part.
I'll draw the years all passing by
So much to learn, so much to try.

I'll paint my mood in shadow blue,
Paint my soul to be with you.
I'll sketch your lips in shaded tones,
Draw your mouth to my own.

I'll trace a hand to wipe your tears
And trace a look to calm your fears.
A silhouette of dark and light
To hold each other oh so tight.

I'll paint the stars in the evening sky,
Draw the light into your eyes,
A touch of love, a touch of grace,
To softly fall on your moonlit face.

And with this ring our lives will start,
Let nothing keep our love apart.
I'll take your hand to hold in mine,
And be together through all time.

David Forster and Arthur Janov

Readings for a civil ceremony

She walks in beauty

She walks in beauty, like the night
Of cloudless climes and starry skies;
And all that's best of dark and bright
   Meet in her aspect and her eyes.
Thus mellowed to that tender light
Which heaven to gaudy day denies.

One shade the more, one ray the less,
Had half impaired the nameless grace
   Which waves in every raven tress,
   Or softly lightens o'er her face;
Where thoughts serenely sweet express
How pure, how dear their dwelling place.

And on that cheek and o'er that brow,
   So soft, so calm, so eloquent,
The smiles that win, the tints that glow,
   But tell of days in goodness spent,
   A mind at peace will all below
   A heart whose love is innocent!

Lord Byron

Love and age

I played with you, mid cowslips blowing,
When I was six and you were four;
When garlands weaving, flower-balls throwing,
Were pleasures soon to please no more.
Through groves and meads, o'er grass and heather,
With little playmates, to and fro,
We wander'd hand in hand together;
But that was sixty years ago.

You grew a lovely roseate maiden,
And still our early love was strong;
Still with no care our days were laden,
They glided joyously along;
And I did love you very dearly,
How dearly words want power to show;
I thought your heart was touch'd as nearly;
But that was fifty years ago.

Then other lovers came around you,
Your beauty grew from year to year,
And many a splendid circle found you
The centre of its glimmering sphere.
I saw you then, first vows forsaking,
On rank and wealth your hand bestow;
O, then I thought my heart was breaking! –
But that was forty years ago.

And I lived on, to wed another:
No cause she gave me to repine;
And when I heard you were a mother,
I did not wish the children mine.

Readings for a civil ceremony

My own young flock, in fair progression,
    Made up a pleasant Christmas row:
My joy in them was past expression;
    But that was thirty years ago.

You grew a matron plump and comely,
    You dwelt in fashion's brightest blaze;
My earthly lot was far more homely;
    But I too had my festal days.
    No merrier eyes have ever glisten'd
    Around the hearth-stone's wintry glow,
Than when my youngest child was christen'd;
    But that was twenty years ago.

Time pass'd. My eldest girl was married,
    And I am now a grandsire gray;
One pet of four years old I've carried
    Among the wild-flower'd meads to play.
In our old fields of childish pleasure,
    Where now, as then, the cowslips blow,
She fills her basket's ample measure;
    And that is not ten years ago.

But though first love's impassion'd blindness
    Has pass'd away in colder light,
I still have thought of you with kindness,
    And shall do, till our last good-night.
    The ever-rolling silent hours
    Will bring a time we shall not know,
When our young days of gathering flowers
    Will be an hundred years ago.

Thomas Love Peacock

Marriage morning

Light, so low upon earth,
You send a flash to the sun.
Here is the golden close of love,
All my wooing is done.
Oh, the woods and the meadows,
Woods where we hid from the wet,
Stiles where we stay'd to be kind,
Meadows in which we met!
Light, so low in the vale
You flash and lighten afar,
For this is the golden morning of love,
And you are his morning start.
Flash, I am coming, I come,
By meadow and stile and wood,
Oh, lighten into my eyes and heart,
Into my heart and my blood!
Heart, are you great enough
For a love that never tires?
O heart, are you great enough for love?
I have heard of thorns and briers,
Over the meadow and stiles,
Over the world to the end of it
Flash for a million miles.

Alfred, Lord Tennyson

The first day

I wish I could remember the first day,
First hour, first moment of your meeting me,
If bright or dim the season it might be
Summer or winter for aught I can say
So unrecorded did it slip away,
So blind was I to see and foresee,
So dull to mark the budding of my tree
That would not blossom yet for many a May.
If only I could recollect it such
A day of days! I let it come and go
As traceless as a thaw of bygone snow;
It seemed to mean so little, meant so much;
If only now I could recall that touch
First touch of hand in hand – did one but know!

Christina Rossetti

The key to love

The key to love is understanding…
The ability to comprehend not only the spoken word
But those unspoken gestures,
The little things that say so much by themselves.

The key to love is forgiveness…
To accept each other's faults and pardon mistakes
Without forgetting, but with remembering
What you learn from them.

The key to love is sharing…
Facing your good fortune as well as the bad, together.
Both conquering problems, forever searching for ways
To intensify your happiness.

The key to love is giving…
Without thought of return,
But with the hope of just a simple smile
And by giving in but never giving up.

The key to love is respect…
Realising that you are two separate people, with different ideas.
That you don't belong to each other,
You belong with each other, and share a mutual bond.

The key to love is inside us all…
It takes time and patience to unlock all the ingredients.
It is the continual learning process that demands a lot of work…
But the rewards are more than worth the effort…
And that is the key to love!

Anon

When you are old

When you are old and grey and full of sleep
And nodding by the fire, take down this book,
And slowly read, and dream of the soft look
Your eyes had once, and of their shadows deep;

How many loved your moments of glad grace,
And loved your beauty with love false or true;
But one man loved the pilgrim soul in you,
And loved the sorrows of your changing face.

And bending down beside the glowing bars,
Murmur, a little sadly, how love fled
And paced upon the mountains overhead,
And hid his face amid a crowd of stars.

W B Yeats

Views on marriage

What greater thing is there than for two human souls than to feel that they are joined for life – to strengthen each other in all labour, to rest on each other in all sorrow, to minister to each other in all pain, to be one with each other in silent, unspeakable memories at the moment of the last parting.
George Eliot

Marriage has in it less of beauty, but more of safety, than the single life; it hath not more ease, but less danger; it is more merry and more sad; it is fuller of sorrows and fuller of joys, it lies under more burdens, but is supported by all the strengths of love and charity; and those burdens are delightful. Marriage is the mother of the world, and preserves kingdoms, and fills cities…
Jeremy Taylor

Kindness is the life's blood, the elixir of marriage. Kindness makes the difference between passion and caring. Kindness is tenderness. Kindness is love, but perhaps greater than love… kindness is good will. Kindness says, 'I want you to be happy.'
Randolph Ray

Two persons who have chosen each other out of all the species, with the design to be each other's mutual comfort and entertainment, have, in that action, bound themselves to be good-humoured, affable, discreet, forgiving, patient, and joyful, with respect to each other's frailties and perfections, to the end of their lives.
Joseph Addison

Chains do not hold a marriage together. It is threads, hundreds of tiny threads which sew people together through the years. That is what makes a marriage last.
Simone Signoret

Readings for a civil ceremony

Marriage lends permanence and a public shape to Love. Marriage vows are made by a man and woman to one another, but they are also made before the world, which is formally present at the ceremony in the role of witness. Marriage solemnises love, giving this most inward of feelings an outward form…

Johnathan Schnell, from The Fate of the Earth

What almost every woman knows sooner or later

Husbands are things that wives have to get used to putting up with.
And with whom they breakfast with and sup with.
They interfere with the discipline of nurseries,
And forget anniversaries,
And when they have been particularly remiss
They think they can cure everything with a great big kiss,
And when you tell them about something awful they have done they just look unbearably patient and smile a superior smile,

And think, Oh she'll get over it after a while.
And they always drink cocktails faster than they can assimilate them,
And if you look in their direction they act as if they were martyrs and you were trying to sacrifice, or immolate them,
And when it's a question of walking five miles to play golf they are very energetic but if it's doing anything useful around the house they are very lethargic,

And then they tell you that women are unreasonable and don't know anything about logic,
And they never want to get up or go to bed at the same time as you do,
And when you perform some simple common or garden rite like putting cold cream on your face or applying a touch of lipstick they seem to think that you are up to some kind of black magic like a priestess of Voodoo.

And they are brave and calm and cool and collected about the ailments of the person they have promised to honour and cherish,
But the minute they get a sniffle or a stomach ache of their own, why you'd think they were about to perish,

And when you are alone with them they ignore all the minor
and as for airs and graces, they utterly lack them,
But when there are a lot of people around they hand you so many chairs
and ashtrays and sandwiches and butter you with such bowings and
scrapings that you want to smack them.

Husbands are indeed an irritating form of life,
And yet through some quirk of Providence most of them are really very
deeply ensconced in the affection of their wife.

Ogden Nash

Quotations and proverbs

Famous sayings, quotations and proverbs about love and marriage are always worth having by your side when thinking about your ceremony and reception. They can be incorporated into your own vows, used as the basis for a reading or as the opening to a speech, or added to an invitation, a menu or a table centre as a romantic literary flourish. Here are some you might like to consider:

Twenty years from now you will be more disappointed by the things that you didn't do than the ones that you did do. So throw off the bowlines. Sail away from the safe harbour. Catch the trade winds in your sails. Explore. Dream. Discover.
Mark Twain

Love is composed of a single soul inhabiting two bodies.
Aristotle

I think a man and woman should choose each other for life, for the simple reason that a long life with all its accidents is barely enough time for a man and woman to understand each other. And... to understand is to love.
W B Yeats

Immature love says 'I love you because I need you';
Mature love says 'I need you because I love you'.
Confucius

Every heart sings a song, incomplete,
until another heart whispers back.
Those who wish to sing always find a song.
At the touch of a lover, everyone becomes a poet.
Plato

When two spiders unite they can tie up a lion.
Ethiopian proverb

Readings for a civil ceremony

The future belongs to those who believe in the beauty of their dreams.
Eleanor Roosevelt

The gold of one's heart is far more precious than the gold of one's purse.
Chinese proverb

Shared joy is a double joy. Shared sorrow is half a sorrow.
Swedish proverb

Don't walk in front of me, I may not follow
Don't walk behind me, I may not lead.
Walk beside me and just be my friend
Irish proverb

No road is long with good company.
Turkish proverb

Anonymous but not forgotten

Many timeless wedding lines and verses have been passed down through the generations until no one really remembers their origin. Here is a selection from unknown sources that may not be attributed to anyone in particular, but they are no less powerful for it:

**Love is like a butterfly.
Hold it too tight and it will crush,
Hold it too loose and it will fly.**

To the world you might be one person,
But to one person you might be the world.

The cure for love is marriage and the cure for marriage is love again.

Let those love now who never loved before,
Let those who always loved, now love the more.

A smile is the light in the window of your face that shows that your heart is home.

A friend is someone who knows all about you and loves you just the same.

**Love is the symbol of eternity, it wipes out all sense of time,
Destroying all memory of a beginning, and all fear of an end.**

May your hands be forever clasped in friendship
And your hearts forever joined in love.

Once in a while, right in the middle of an ordinary life, love gives us a fairy tale.

To love a person is to learn the song that is in their heart,
and sing it to them when they have forgotten.

Readings for a civil ceremony

A moment of mirth

Weddings may be all hearts and flowers, but they can also be a source of amusement. Some writers can be as witty as they are wise and it is their ability to look at even the most important day with a tongue firmly in their cheek that offers modern couples the chance to incorporate some more light-hearted musings into their special occasion.

Marriage is the triumph of imagination over intelligence.
Second marriage is the triumph of hope over experience.
Oscar Wilde

My advice to you is to get married.
If you find a good wife, you'll be happy.
If not, you'll become a philosopher.
Socrates

Strange to say what delight we married people have to see these poor fools decoyed into our condition!
Samuel Pepys

Marriage is the result of the longing for the deep peace of the double bed after the hurly-burly of the chaise-longue.
Attributed to Mrs Patrick Campbell

He tells you when you've got on too much lipstick,
And helps you with your girdle when your hips stick.
Ogden Nash in The Perfect Husband

Marriages are made in heaven –
but then so are thunder, lightning, tornados and hail.
Anon

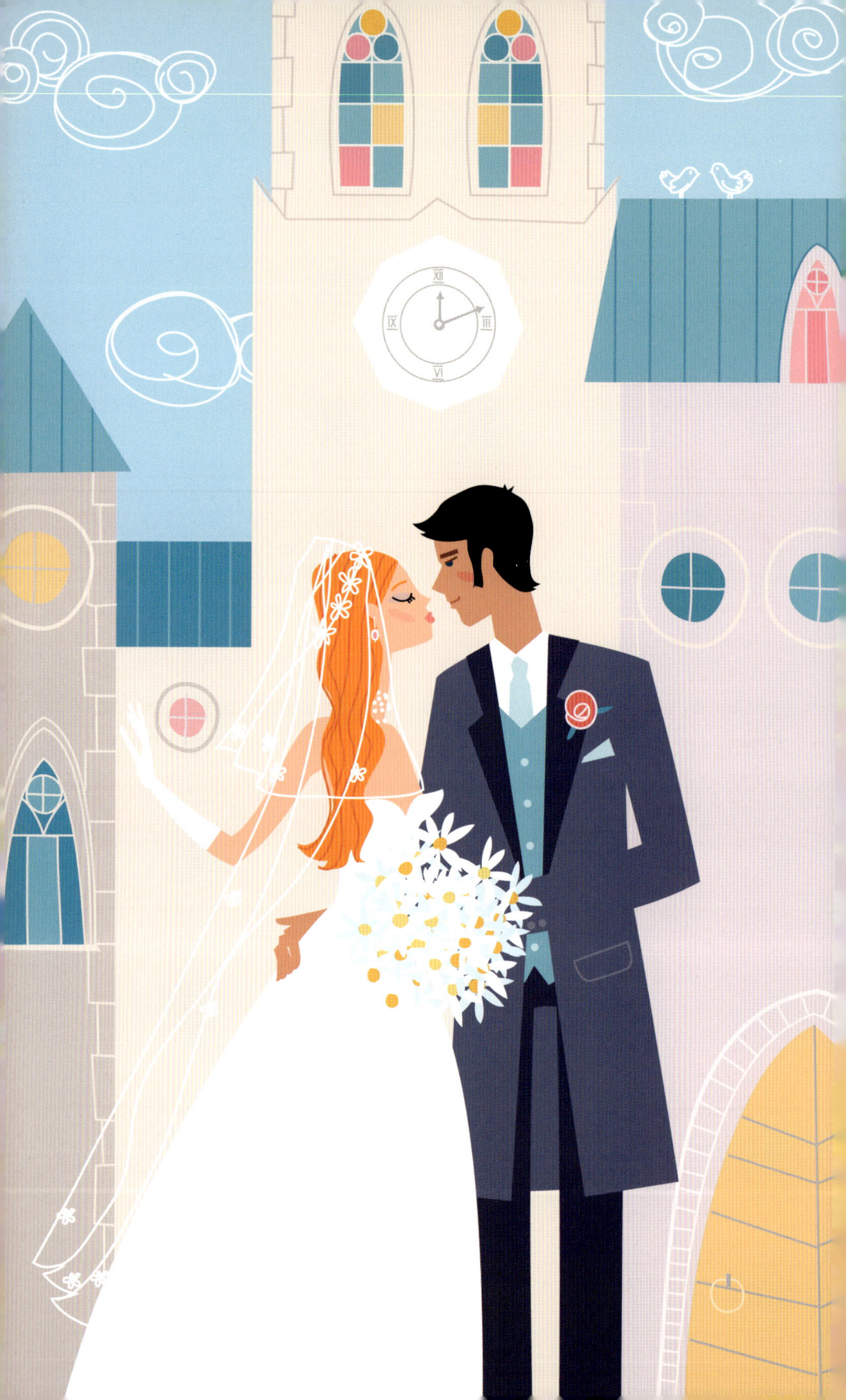

Chapter 5

Readings for a religious ceremony

A religious wedding is the most formal type of ceremony and includes a selection of readings that say something meaningful about your faith, as well as the importance of marriage.

Inspiration for readings at a traditional Christian wedding is likely to come from the Bible, although your vicar or priest may be happy for you to include a reading about love or marriage providing it still sets the right solemn tone: for example, Shakespeare or classical love poetry.

Your officiant will be happy to help you with ideas and will probably give you a list of readings that have been popular at other weddings. This is a good place to start, but don't feel you have to choose one of these. You might have your own favourite Bible passage or you could, for example, choose the same readings used at your parents' wedding ceremony.

Take time to read through the text carefully, making sure that it feels appropriate to you both. When you have narrowed down a few options, have a go at reading them aloud to see if the words flow and create the right tone for what you had in mind. Don't feel you have to make any reading too long; one or two minutes of spoken text is about right, which equates to between 250 and 400 written words. As with anything you want to include as part of your wedding ceremony, give your minister or priest a list of preferences well in advance for approval. If it proves necessary to make any changes, you will still have plenty of time to find alternatives.

Bible readings from the Old Testament

(All from the New International Version. See website www.ibs.org.)

God creates woman for man (Genesis 2: 18–24)

Then the Lord God said, 'It is not good that the man should be alone; I will make him a helper as his partner.'

So out of the ground the Lord God formed every animal of the field and every bird of the air, and brought them to the man to see what he would call them; and whatever the man called each living creature, that was its name.

The man gave names to all the cattle, and to the birds of the air, and to every animal of the field, but for the man there was not found a helper as his partner.

So the Lord God caused a deep sleep to fall upon the man, and he slept; then he took one of his ribs and closed up its place with flesh.

And the rib that the Lord God had taken from the man he made into a woman and brought her to the man.

Then the man said, 'This at last is bone of my bones and flesh of my flesh; this one shall be called woman, for out of Man this one was taken.'

Therefore a man leaves his father and mother and clings to his wife, and they become one flesh.

Readings for a religious ceremony

For everything a season (Ecclesiastes 3: 1–8)

There is a time for everything, and a season for every activity under heaven:

A time to be born and a time to die; a time to plant and a time to uproot;

A time to kill and a time to heal; a time to tear down and a time to build;

A time to weep and a time to laugh; a time to mourn and a time to dance;

A time to scatter stones and a time to gather them; a time to embrace and a time to refrain;

A time to search and a time to give up; a time to keep and a time to throw away;

A time to tear and a time to mend; a time to be silent and a time to speak;

A time to love and a time to hate; a time for war and a time for peace.

Two are better than one (Ecclesiastes 4: 9–12)

Two are better than one, because they have a good return for their work. If one falls down, his friend can help him up. But pity the man who falls and has no-one to help him up!

Also, if two lie down together, they will keep warm. But how can one keep warm alone!

Though one may be overpowered, two can defend themselves.

A good wife (Proverbs 31: 10–31)

A wife of noble character who can find? She is worth far more than rubies.
Her husband has full confidence in her and lacks nothing of value.
She brings him good, not harm, all the days of her life.
She selects wool and flax and works with eager hands.
She is like the merchant ships, bringing her food from afar.
She gets up while it is still dark; she provides food for her family and portions for her servant girls.
She considers a field and buys it; out of her earnings she plants a vineyard.
She sets about her work vigorously; her arms are strong for her tasks.
She sees that her trading is profitable, and her lamp does not go out at night.
In her hand she holds the distaff and grasps the spindle with her fingers.
She opens her arms to the poor and extends her hands to the needy.
When it snows, she has no fear for her household; for all of them are clothed in scarlet.
She makes coverings for her bed; she is clothed in fine linen and purple.
Her husband is respected at the city gate, where he takes his seat among the elders of the land.
She makes linen garments and sells them, and supplies the merchants with sashes.
She is clothed with strength and dignity; she can laugh at the days to come.
She speaks with wisdom, and faithful instruction is on her tongue.
She watches over the affairs of her household and does not eat the bread of idleness.
Her children arise and call her blessed; her husband also, and he praises her:
'Many women do noble things, but you surpass them all.'
Charm is deceptive, and beauty is fleeting; but a woman who fears the Lord is to be praised.
Give her the reward she has earned, and let her works bring her praise at the city gate.

Readings for a religious ceremony

Promise of hope (Jeremiah 33: 10–11)

The Lord said 'People are saying that this place is like a desert, that it has no people or animals living in it. And they are right: the towns of Judah and the streets of Jerusalem are empty; no people or animals live there. But in these places you will hear again the shouts of gladness and joy and the happy sounds of wedding feasts.

You will hear people sing as they bring thank offerings to my Temple; they will say, 'Give thanks to the Lord Almighty, because he is good and his love is eternal.' I will make this land as prosperous as it was before, I, the Lord, have spoken.

I will make you my wife (Hosea 2: 19)

I will make you my wife, I will be true and faithful; I will show you constant love and mercy and make you mine forever.

Clothed in salvation (Isaiah 61: 10–11)

I will greatly rejoice in the Lord; my soul shall exult in my God, for he has clothed me with the garments of salvation; he has covered me with the robe of righteousness, as a bridegroom decks himself like a priest with a beautiful headdress, and as a bride adorns herself with her jewels.

For as the earth brings forth its sprouts, and as a garden causes what is sown in it to sprout up, so the Lord God will cause righteousness and praise to sprout up before all the nations.

Let us sing to the Lord (Psalm 95: 1–7)

Come, let us sing for joy to the Lord; let us make a joyful noise to the rock of our salvation!
Let us come into his presence with thanksgiving and extol him with music and song.
For the Lord is the great God, the great King above all gods.
In his hand are the depths of the earth, and the mountain peaks belong to him.
The sea is his, for he made it, and his hands formed the dry land.
Come, let us bow down in worship, let us kneel before the Lord, our Maker;
For he is our God and we are the people of his pasture, the flock under his care.

His steadfast love endures forever (Psalm 136: 1–9)

Give thanks to the Lord, for he is good, for his steadfast love endures forever.
Give thanks to the God of gods, for his steadfast love endures forever.
Give thanks to the Lord of lords, for his steadfast love endures forever;
To him who alone does great wonders, for his steadfast love endures forever;
To him who by understanding made the heavens, for his steadfast love endures forever;
To him who spread out the earth above the waters, for his steadfast love endures forever;
To him who made the great lights, for his steadfast love endures forever;
The sun to rule over the day, for his steadfast love endures forever;
The moon and stars to rule over the night, for his steadfast love endures forever.

Readings for a religious ceremony

God is our refuge and strength
(Psalm 46)

God is our refuge and strength, a very present help in trouble.

Therefore we will not fear, though the earth should change, though the mountains shake in the heart of the sea; though its waters roar and foam, though the mountains tremble with its tumult. There is a river whose streams make glad the city of God, the holy habitations of the Most High.

God is in the midst of the city; it shall not be moved; God will help it when the morning dawns.

The nations are in an uproar, the kingdoms totter; he utters his voice, the earth melts.

The Lord of hosts is with us; the God of Jacob is our refuge.

Come, behold the works of the Lord; see what desolations he has brought on the earth.

He makes wars cease to the end of the earth; he breaks the bow, and shatters the spear; he burns the shields with fire.

'Be still, and know that I am God! I am exalted among the nations, I am exalted in the earth.'

The Lord of hosts is with us; the God of Jacob is our refuge.

May God be gracious (Psalm 67)

May God be gracious to us and bless us and make his face to shine upon us, that your way may be known on earth, your saving power among all nations. Let the peoples praise you, O God; let all the peoples praise you! Let the nations be glad and sing for joy, for you judge the peoples with equity and guide the nations upon earth. Let the peoples praise you, O God; let all the peoples praise you! The earth has yielded its increase; God, our God, shall bless us. May God continue to bless us; let all the ends of the earth revere him!

I lift up my eyes to the hills (Psalm 121)

I lift up my eyes to the hills. From where does my help come? My help comes from the Lord, who made heaven and earth. He will not let your foot be moved; he who keeps you will not slumber.
Behold, he who keeps Israel will neither slumber nor sleep. The Lord is your keeper; the Lord is your shade on your right hand. The sun shall not strike you by day, nor the moon by night. The Lord will keep you from all evil; he will keep your life. The Lord will keep your going out and your coming in from this time and forever more.

Readings for a religious ceremony

The constancy of Ruth
(Ruth 1: 16–17)

But Ruth said; 'Do not press me to leave you or to turn back from following you! Where you go, I will go; where you lodge, I will lodge; your people shall be my people, and your God my God.

'Where you die, I will die – there will I be buried. May the Lord do thus and so to me, and more as well, if even death parts me from you!'

Love is as strong as death
(The Song of Solomon 8: 6–7)

Set me as a seal upon your heart, as a seal upon your arm; for love is strong as death, passion fierce as the grave. Its flashes are flashes of fire, a raging flame.

Many waters cannot quench love, neither can floods drown it. If one offered for love all the wealth of one's house, it would be utterly scorned.

Bible readings from the New Testament

Love (I Corinthians 13: 4–13)

Love is patient, love is kind. It does not envy,
it does not boast, it is not proud.
It is not rude, it is not self-seeking, it is not easily angered,
it keeps no record of wrongs.
Love does not delight in evil but rejoices with the truth.
It always protects, always trusts, always hopes, always perseveres.
Love never fails. But where there are prophecies, they will cease; where there are tongues, they will be stilled; where there is knowledge,
it will pass away.
For we know in part and we prophesy in part, but when perfection comes, the imperfect disappears.
When I was a child, I talked like a child, I thought like a child, I reasoned like a child. When I became a man, I put childish ways behind me.
Now we see but a poor reflection as in a mirror; then we shall see face to face. Now I know in part; then I shall know fully,
even as I am fully known.
And now these three remain: faith, hope and love. But the greatest of these is love.

Put on love which binds everything together in harmony (Colossians 3: 12–14)

Therefore, as God's chosen people, holy and dearly loved, clothe yourselves with compassion, kindness, humility, gentleness and patience.
Bear with each other and forgive whatever grievances you may have against one another. Forgive as the Lord forgave you.
And over all these virtues put on love, which binds them all together in perfect unity.

Wives submit to your husbands, husbands love your wives
(Ephesians 5: 22–33)

Wives, submit to your husbands as to the Lord. For the husband is the head of the wife as Christ is the head of the church, his body, of which he is the Saviour.

Now as the church submits to Christ, so also wives should submit to their husbands in everything.

Husbands, love your wives, just as Christ loved the church and gave himself up for her to make her holy, cleansing her by the washing with water through the word, and to present her to himself as a radiant church, without stain or wrinkle or any other blemish, but holy and blameless.

In this same way, husbands ought to love their wives as their own bodies. He who loves his wife loves himself.

After all, no one ever hated his own body, but he feeds and cares for it, just as Christ does the church, for we are members of his body.

'For this reason a man will leave his father and mother and be united to his wife, and the two will become one flesh.'

This is a profound mystery – but I am talking about Christ and the church.

However, each one of you also must love his wife as he loves himself, and the wife must respect her husband.

I am the vine and you are the branches
(John 15: 1–8)

I am the true vine, and my Father is the gardener.
He cuts off every branch in me that bears no fruit, while every branch that does bear fruit he prunes so that it will be even more fruitful.
You are already clean because of the word I have spoken to you.
Remain in me, and I will remain in you. No branch can bear fruit by itself; it must remain in the vine. Neither can you bear fruit unless you remain in me.
I am the vine; you are the branches. If a man remains in me and I in him, he will bear much fruit; apart from me you can do nothing.
If anyone does not remain in me, he is like a branch that is thrown away and withers; such branches are picked up, thrown into the fire and burned.
If you remain in me and my words remain in you, ask whatever you wish, and it will be given you.
This is to my Father's glory, that you bear much fruit, showing yourselves to be my disciples.

The Sermon on the Mount (Matthew 5: 1–10)

Seeing the crowds, he went up on the mountain, and when he sat down, his disciples came to him.
And he opened his mouth and taught them, saying:
'Blessed are the poor in spirit, for theirs is the kingdom of heaven.
'Blessed are those who mourn, for they shall be comforted.
'Blessed are the meek, for they shall inherit the earth.
'Blessed are those who hunger and thirst for righteousness, for they shall be satisfied.
'Blessed are the merciful, for they shall receive mercy.
'Blessed are the pure in heart, for they shall see God.
'Blessed are the peacemakers, for they shall be called sons of God.
'Blessed are those who are persecuted for righteousness' sake, for theirs is the kingdom of heaven.'

Readings for a religious ceremony

Love one another as I have loved you
(John 15: 9–17)

As the Father has loved me, so have I loved you. Now remain in my love. If you obey my commands, you will remain in my love, just as I have obeyed my Father's commands and remain in his love.

I have told you this so that my joy may be in you and that your joy may be complete.

My command is this: Love each other as I have loved you.

Greater love has no one than this, that he lay down his life for his friends. You are my friends if you do what I command.

I no longer call you servants, because a servant does not know his master's business. Instead, I have called you friends, for everything that I learned from my Father I have made known to you.

You did not choose me, but I chose you and appointed you to go and bear fruit – fruit that will last. Then the Father will give you whatever you ask in my name.

This is my command: love each other.

Let love be genuine (Romans 12: 9–12)

Love must be sincere. Hate what is evil; cling to what is good.
Be devoted to one another in brotherly love. Honour one another above yourselves.
Never be lacking in zeal, but keep your spiritual fervour, serving the Lord.
Be joyful in hope, patient in affliction, faithful in prayer.

Readings for a Jewish ceremony

Reading from the Talmut (Ketubot 8)

Blessed art thou, O Lord, King of the Universe, who created mirth and joy, bridegroom and bride, gladness, jubilation dancing, and delight, love and brotherhood, peace and fellowship. Quickly, O Lord our God, may the sound of mirth and joy be heard in the streets of Judah and Jerusalem, the voice of bridegroom and bride, jubilant voices of bridegroom from their canopies and youths from the feasts of song. Blessed art though, O Lord, who makes the bridegroom rejoice with the bride.

Readings for a religious ceremony

The Seven Blessings

We acknowledge the Unity of all within the sovereignty of God, expressing our appreciation for this wine, symbol and aid of our rejoicing.

We acknowledge the Unity of all within the sovereignty of God, realising that each separate moment and every distinct object points to and shares in this oneness.

We acknowledge the Unity of all within the sovereignty of God, recognising and appreciating the blessing of being human.

We acknowledge the Unity of all within the sovereignty of God, realising the special gift of awareness that permits us to perceive this unity and the wonder we experience as a man and a woman joined to live together.

May rejoicing resound throughout the world as the homeless are given homes, persecution and oppression cease, and all people learn to live in peace with each other and in harmony with their environment.

From the Divine, source of all energy, we call forth an abundance of love to envelop this couple. May they be for each other lovers and friends, and may their love partake of the same innocence, purity, and sense of discovery that we imagine the first couple to have experienced.

We acknowledge the Unity of all within the sovereignty of God, and we highlight today joy and gladness, bridegroom and bride, delight and cheer, love and harmony, peace and companionship. May we all witness the day when the dominant sounds through the world will be these sounds of happiness, the voices of lovers, the sounds of feasting and singing.

Praised is love; blessed be this marriage. May the bride and bridegroom rejoice together.

Anita Diamant, from The New Jewish Wedding

Traditional poetry and prose for a religious wedding

Providing there are no religious connotations, many of these are also suitable for inclusion in a civil wedding ceremony.

Marriage is a commitment

Marriage is a commitment to take that joy deep, deeper than happiness deep into the discovery of who you most truly are. It is a commitment to a spiritual journey, to a life of becoming – in which joy can comprehend despair; running through rivers of pain into joy again.

Thus marriage is even deeper than commitment. It is a covenant – a covenant that says: I love you – I trust you – I will be here for you when you are hurting, and when I am hurting I will not leave. It is a covenant intended not to provide a haven from pain or anger or sorrow. Life offers no such haven. Instead marriage is intended to provide a sanctuary safe enough to risk loving; to risk living and sharing from the centre of oneself. This is worth everything.

Anon

Readings for a religious ceremony

Marriage joins two people in the circle of its love

Marriage is a commitment to life, the best that two people can find and bring out in each other. It offers opportunities for sharing and growth that no other relationship can equal. It is a physical and an emotional joining that is promised for a lifetime.

Within the circle of its love, marriage encompasses all of life's most important relationships. A wife and a husband are each other's best friend, confidant, lover, teacher, listener and critic. And there may come times when one partner is heartbroken or ailing, and the love of the other may resemble the tender caring of a parent for a child.

Marriage deepens and enriches every facet of life. Happiness is fuller, memories are fresher, commitment is stronger, even anger is felt more strongly, and passes away more quickly.

Marriage understands and forgives the mistakes life is unable to avoid. It encourages and nurtures new life, new experiences, and new ways of expressing love that is deeper than life.

When two people pledge their love and care for each other in marriage, they create a spirit unique unto themselves which binds them closer than any spoken or written words. Marriage is a promise, a potential made in the hearts of two people who love each other and takes a lifetime to fulfil.

Edmund O'Neill

Marriage is one long conversation

Marriage is one long conversation, chequered by disputes. The disputes are valueless; they but ingrain the difference; the heroic heart of woman prompting her at once to nail her colours to the mast. But in the intervals, almost unconsciously, and with no desire to shine, the whole material of life is turned over and over, ideas are struck out and shared, the two persons more and more adapt their notions one to suit the other, and in the process of time, without sound of trumpet, they conduct each other into new worlds of thought.

Robert Louis Stevenson

The path of marriage

The meaning of marriage begins in the giving of words. We cannot join ourselves to one another without giving, for in joining ourselves to one another we join ourselves to the unknown. We can join one another only by joining the unknown. We must not be misled by the procedures of experimental thought: in life, in the world, we are never given two known results to choose between, but only one result that we choose without knowing what it is…

Because the condition of marriage is worldly and its meaning communal, no one party to it can be solely in charge. What you alone think it ought to be, it is not going to be. Where you alone think you want it to go, it is not going to go. It is going where the two of you – and marriage, time, history and the world – will take it. You do not know the road, you have committed your life to a way.

Wendell Berry, extracted from 'Poetry on marriage' from Standing by Words

Readings for a religious ceremony

Marriage

Love one another, but make not a bond of love:
Let it rather be a moving sea between the shores of your souls.
Fill each other's cup but drink not from one cup.
Give one another of your bread but eat not from the same loaf.
Sing and dance together and be joyous, but let each one of you be alone.
Even as the strings of a lute are alone though they quiver with the same music.
Give your hearts, but not into each other's keeping.
For only the hand of life can contain your hearts.
And stand together yet not too near together:
For the pillars of the temple stand apart,
And the Oak tree and the Cypress grow not in each other's shadow.

Kahlil Gibran

A marriage

Makes of two fractional lives a whole;
It gives to two purposeless lives a work
And doubles the strength of each to perform it
It gives to two questioning natures a reason for living,
And something to live for;
It will give a new gladness to the sunshine,
A new fragrance to the flowers,
A new beauty to the earth,
And a new mystery to life.

Mark Twain

Marriage is…

Marriage is a dynamic process of discovery,
Marriage is a journey, not an arrival.
In marriage, being the right person is as important as finding the right person.
Marriage is starting to love, over and over again.
Marriage is a life's work.
Marriage is an art… and like any creative process,
It requires active thought and effort.
We have to learn how to share on many different levels.
We need to practise talking from the heart,
And understanding attitudes as well as words.
Giving generously and receiving graciously are talents that are available to anyone.
But all these skills need to be developed, if the marriage picture that we paint
is to be anything approaching the masterpiece intended.

Anon

Readings for a religious ceremony

The sanctity of marriage

God is guiding your marriage. Marriage is more than your love for each other. It has a higher dignity and power, for it is God's holy ordinance, through which he wills to perpetuate the human race till the end of time. In your love you see only your two selves in the world, but in marriage you are a link in the chain of the generations, which God causes to come and to pass away to his glory, and calls into his kingdom. In your love you see only the heaven of your own happiness, but in marriage you are placed at a post of responsibility towards the world and mankind. Your love is your own private possession, but marriage is more than something personal – it is a status, an office.

Just as it is the crown, and not merely the will to rule, that makes the king, so it is marriage, and not merely your love for each other, that joins you together in the sight of God and man. As you first gave the ring to one another and have now received it a second time from the hand of the pastor, so love comes from you, but marriage from above, from God. As high as God is above man, so high are the sanctity, the rights, and the promise of marriage above the sanctity, the rights, and the promise of love. It is not your love that sustains the marriage, but from now on, the marriage that sustains your love.

Dietrich Bonhoeffer

A walled garden

'Your marriage', he said, 'should have within it, a secret and protected place open to you alone. Imagine it to be a walled garden, entered by a door to which you only hold the key.

'Within this garden you will cease to be a mother, father, employee, homemaker or any other of the roles which you fulfil in daily life. Here you are yourselves two people who love each other. Here you can concentrate on one another's needs.

'So take my hand and let us go back to our garden. The time we spend together is not wasted but invested. Invested in our future and the nurture of our love.'

Anon

Readings for a religious ceremony

To my dear loving husband

If ever two were one, then surely we.
If ever man were loved by wife, then thee;
If ever wife was happy in a man,
Compare with me, ye woman, if you can.
I prize thy love more than whole mines of gold
Or all the riches that the East doth hold.
My love is such that rivers cannot quench
Nor ought but love from thee, give recompense.
Thy love is such I can no way repay
The heavens reward thee manifold, I pray
The while we live, in love let's so persevere
That when we live no more, we may live ever.

Anne Bradstreet

Marriage is the beginning of an enterprise

Marriage is the beginning of an enterprise. In theory, two people have decided they love and trust and respect each other well enough to want to spend the rest of their lives together. They will build something that appears to outsiders something infinitely simple, but which in fact, is infinitely complex – an ark to survive all weathers.

In reality, of course, people blunder into marriage for a dozen reasons – and often spend the rest of their lives on a disintegrating raft, held together with pieces of string. But any craft will stay afloat as long as its builders are happier to share its limitations than risk sharks. A boat can be merely a means of survival – or a means to a great discovery. Its course may be erratic, the repairs to its structure constant and haphazard – but if it is still afloat it has, with all its eccentricities, a jaunty air, a lived-in look, an air of comfortable companionship.

Pam Brown, from Happy Anniversary

Sonnet 116

Let me not to the marriage of true minds
Admit impediments. Love is not love
Which alters when it alteration finds,
Or bends with the remover to remove:
O, no! It is an ever-fix'd mark,
That looks on tempests and is never shaken;
It is the star to every wandering bark,
Whose worth's unknown, although his height be taken.
Love's not Time's fool, though rosy lips and cheeks
Within his bending sickle's compass come;
Love alters not with his brief hours and weeks,
But bears it out even to the edge of doom.
If this be error and upon me prov'd,
I never writ, nor no man ever lov'd.

William Shakespeare

Intimacy and fidelity in marriage

The movement into marriage involves the risks of intimacy. In marriage I must be able to come close to you in a way that lets you know and influence me. I must face the risk of being changed, of coming to a different awareness of who I am as a result of our life together. I must accept the responsibility of my own influence in your life as well. Intimacy involves an overlapping of space, a willingness to be influenced, and openness to the possibility of change. It invites me beyond myself…

Fidelity is the virtue of the core of the lifelong commitment of marriage. In the phrase 'lifelong commitment' we begin to glimpse the complexity of this virtue: commitment suggests stability and lifelong implies changes… Marital fidelity combines commitment and change as two persons seek to grow in the same direction; fidelity is the careful tending of both the commitments and the changes necessary in a maturing love.

Evelyn and James Whitehead, from Marrying Well

Marriage advice

Let your love be stronger than your hate or anger. Learn the wisdom of compromise, for it is better to bend a little than to break. Believe the best rather than the worst. People have a way of living up or down to your opinion of them. Remember that true friendship is the basis for any lasting relationship. The person you choose to marry is deserving of the courtesies and kindnesses you bestow on your friends. Please hand this down to your children and your children's children.

Jane Wells

Readings for a religious ceremony

Why marriage?

Because to the depths of me, I long to love one person,
With all my heart, my soul, my mind, my body...

Because I need a forever friend to trust with the intimacies of me,
Who won't hold them against me,
Who loves me when I'm unlikable,
Who sees the small child in me, and
Who looks for the divine potential of me...

Because I need to cuddle in the warmth of the night
With someone who thanks God for me,
With someone I feel blessed to hold...

Because marriage means opportunity
To grow in love in friendship...

Because marriage is a discipline
To be added to a list of achievements...
Because marriages do not fail, people fail
When they enter into marriage
Expecting another to make them whole...

Because, knowing this,
I promise myself to take full responsibility
For my spiritual, mental and physical wholeness
I create me,
I take half of the responsibility for my marriage
Together we create our marriage...

Because with this understanding
The possibilities are limitless.

Mari Nichols-Haining

Traditional Irish blessing

May the road rise to meet you,
May the wind be always at your back.
May the sun shine warm upon your face,
The rains fall soft upon your fields.
And until we meet again,
May God hold you in the palm of his hand.

May God be with you and bless you;
May you see your children's children.
May you be poor in misfortune,
Rich in blessings,
May you know nothing but happiness
From this day forward.

May the road rise to meet you
May the wind be always at your back
May the warm rays of sun fall upon your home
And may the hand of a friend always be near.

May green be the grass you walk on,
May blue be the skies above you,
May pure be the joys that surround you,
May true be the hearts that love you.

Anon

Readings for a religious ceremony

A marriage prayer

Bless this marriage, O God, as they begin their
journey down the road of life together.

We don't know what lies ahead for the road turns and bends. But help them to make the best of whatever comes their way.

Help them to hug each other often… laugh a lot, talk more, and argue less.

Help them to continue to enjoy each other as they did when they first met.

Help them to realise that nothing nor no one is perfect and to look for the good in all things and all people, including themselves.

Help them to respect each other's likes and dislikes, opinion and beliefs, hopes and dreams and fears even though they may not always understand them.

Help them to learn from each other and to help each other to grow mentally, emotionally, and spiritually.

Help them to realise that there is design and purpose in their lives as in the world and no matter what happens to them they will hold on to each other and know that things have a way of working out for the good.

Help them to create for their children a peaceful, stable home of love as a foundation on which they can build their lives.

But most of all, dear God, help them to keep lit the torch of love that they now share in their hearts so that by their loving example they may pass on the light of love to their children and to their children's children forever. *Amen*

Bud Henry Bowen

On love

The love of God, unutterable and perfect,
Flows into a pure soul the way that light
Rushes into a transparent object.
The more love that it finds, the more it gives itself,
So that, as we grow more clear and open,
The more complete the joy of loving is.
And the more the souls, who resonate together,
The greater the intensity of their love
For, mirror-like, each soul reflects the others.

Dante

Readings for a religious ceremony

On love and relationships

When you love someone, you do not love them all the time, in exactly the same way, from moment to moment. It is an impossibility. It is even a lie to pretend to. And yet this is exactly what most of us demand. We have so little faith in the ebb and flow of life, of love, of relationships. We leap at the flow of the tide and resist in terror its ebb. We are afraid it will never return. We insist on permanency, on duration, on continuity; when the only continuity possible, in life as in love, is in growth, in fluidity – in freedom, in the sense that the dancers are free, barely touching as they pass, but partners in the same pattern.

The only real security is not in owning or possessing, not in demanding or expecting, not in hoping, even. Security in a relationship lies neither in looking back to what was in nostalgia, nor forward to what it might be in dread or anticipation, but living in the present relationship and accepting it as it is now. Relationships must be like islands, one must accept them for what they are here and now, within their limits – islands, surrounded and interrupted by the sea, and continually visited and abandoned by the tides…

It takes years to marry completely two hearts, even of the most loving and well assorted. A happy wedlock is a long falling in love. Young persons think love belongs only to the brown-haired and crimson-cheeked. So it does for its beginning. But the golden marriage is a part of love which the Bridal day knows nothing of…

Such a large and sweet fruit is a complete marriage that it needs a long summer to ripen, and then a long winter to mellow and season it. But a really happy marriage of love and judgement between a noble man and woman is one of the things so very handsome that if the sun were, as the Greek poets fabled, a God, he might stop the world and hold it still now and then in order to look all day long on some example thereof, and feast his eyes on such a spectacle.

Anne Morrow Lindbergh

There is no happier life but in a wife

There is no happier life
But in a wife,
The comforts are so sweet
When two do meet.
'Tis plenty, peace, a calm
Like dropping balm;
Love's weather is so fair,
Like perfumed air.
Each word such pleasure brings
Life soft-touched strings;
Love's passion moves the heart
On either part;
Such harmony together,
So pleased in either.
No discords; concords still,
Sealed with one will.
By love, God made man one,
Yet not alone.
Like stamps of king and queen
It may be seen.
Two figures on one coin,
So do they join,
Only they not embrace,
We, face to face.
William Cavendish

Readings for a religious ceremony

How do I love thee?

How do I love thee? Let me count the ways.
I love thee to the depth and breadth and height
My soul can reach, when feeling out of sight
For the ends of Being and ideal Grace.
I love thee to the level of every day's
Most quiet need, by sun and candlelight.
I love thee freely, as men strive for Right;
I love thee purely, as they turn from Praise.
I love with a passion put to use
In my old griefs, and with my childhood's faith.
I love thee with a love I seemed to lose
With my lost saints, – I love thee with the breath,
Smiles, tears, of all my life! – and, if God choose,
I shall but love thee better after death.

Elizabeth Barrett Browning

Love's philosophy

The fountains mingle with the river,
And the rivers with the ocean;
The winds of heaven mix forever
With a sweet emotion;
Nothing in the world is single:
All things by a law divine
In another's being mingle–
Why not I with thine?

See, the mountains kiss high heaven,
And the waves clasp one another;
No sister flower could be forgiven
If it disdained its brother;
And the sunlight clasps the earth,
And the moonbeams kiss the sea;–
What are all these kissings worth,
If thou kiss not me?

Percy Bysshe Shelley

Readings for a religious ceremony

Love and being in love

Being in love is a good thing, but it is not the best thing. There are many things below it, but there are also things above it. You cannot make it the basis of a whole life. It is a noble feeling, but it is still a feeling… who could bear to live in that excitement for even five years?… But, of course, ceasing to 'be in love' need not mean ceasing to love. Love in a second sense – love as distinct from 'being in love' – is not merely a feeling. It is a deep unity, maintained by will and deliberately strengthened by habit; reinforced by the grace which both parents ask, and receive, from God. They can have this love for each other even at those moments when they do not like each other; as you love yourself even when you do not like yourself. They can retain this love even when each would easily, if they allowed themselves, be 'in love' with someone else. 'Being in love' first moved them to promise fidelity: this quieter love enables them to keep the promise. It is on this love that the engine of marriage is run; being in love was the explosion that started it.

C S Lewis

Peace and love

Peace does not come through the agreement of egos, for it is impossible for egos to agree. Peace comes when love and mutual respect are present. When love is present, your enemy becomes like a friend who is not afraid to disagree with you. You do not cast him out of your heart just because he sees things differently from you. You listen carefully to what he has to say.

When you listen to your enemy the same way that you would listen to your friend, it is not your ego doing the listening. The Spirit inside of you is listening to the Spirit inside of him.

The cause of all human conflict is a simple one: each side dehumanises the other. Each side sees the other as less worthy. As long as each side perceives the other this way, even the simplest details cannot be negotiated. But let each side bring to the other the attitude of respect and acceptance, and even difficult details will be resolved.

Miracles come from love. The solutions that come from loving minds are without limit. The willingness to love – to regard each other as equals – is the essence behind all miracle making.

Paul Ferrine, from Love Without Conditions

Readings for a religious ceremony

My true love

My true love hath my heart and I have his,
By just exchange one for another given
I hold his dear, and mine he cannot miss,
There never was a better bargain driven
My true love hath my heart and I have his.

His heart in me keeps him and me in one,
My heart in him his thoughts and senses guides
He loves my heart, for once it was his own,
I cherish his because in me it bides
My true love hath my heart and I have his.

Sir Phillip Sydney

True love

True love is a sacred flame
That burns eternally,
And none can dim its special glow
Or change its destiny.
True love speaks in tender tones
And hears with gentle ear,
True love gives with open heart
And true love conquers fear.
True love makes no harsh demands
It neither rules nor binds,
And true love holds with gentle hands
The hearts that it entwines.

Anon

'Til death us do part

I hope it is decades before death parts us
But I don't know what God has in mind
I pray that he'll let us be happy always
But I can't comprehend plans divine.

It may be that turmoil will dot our landscape
With its grey skies and swirling intrusion
It may be that joy will fill both our hearts
And we'll think pain is just an illusion.

But I think it's likely we'll see some of each
As we walk on this pathway together
I promise you now: I will give all I have
From my mouth you'll not hear the word 'Never.'

With so much uncertainty, crime, and abuse
That exists, everywhere, all around us
More than ever we need to hold fast to the truth
Of our marriage…Life will not confound us.

Time together is fleeting; it is too scarce to waste
My goal is to make my life-mission
A beautiful tapestry highlighting 'us'
Sewn with threads from our human condition.

I want to explore the full spectrum of life
Before we're too close to its leaving
I want to embrace vast explosions of joy
That make both our hearts strong and heaving.

I know I will love you for all of my life
No matter the time we are given.
I'm your till death parts us – left all alone –
Until God reunites us in heaven.

Carol D Bos

Readings for a religious ceremony

Learning to love

One must learn to love, and go through a good deal of suffering to get to it, like any knight of the grail, and the journey is always towards the other soul, not away from it. Do you think love is an accomplished thing, the day it is recognised? It isn't. To love, you have to learn to understand the other, more than she understands herself, and to submit to her understanding of you. It is damnably difficult and painful, but is the only thing which endures. You mustn't think that your desire or your fundamental need is to make a good career, or to fill your life with activity, or even to provide for your family materially. It isn't. Your most vital necessity in this life is that you shall love your wife completely and implicitly and in entire nakedness of body and spirit. Then you will have peace and inner security, no matter how many things go wrong.

D H Lawrence, from Selected Letters

Prayers and blessings for marriage

Blessing for a marriage

May your marriage bring you all the exquisite excitements a marriage should bring, and may life grant you also patience, tolerance, and understanding.

May you always need one another – not so much to fill your emptiness as to help you know your fullness.

A mountain needs a valley to be complete; the valley does not make the mountain less but more; and the valley is more a valley because it has a mountain towering over it.

So let it be with you and you.

May you need one another, but not out of weakness.
May you want one another, but not out of lack.
May you entice one another, but not compel one another.
May you succeed in all important ways with one another, and not fail in the little graces.
May you look for things to praise, often say, 'I love you!' and take no notice of small faults.
If you have quarrels that push you apart, may both of you hope to have good sense enough to take the first step back.

May you enter into the mystery which is the awareness of one another's presence – no more physical than spiritual, warm and near when you are side by side, and warm and near when you are in separate rooms or even distant cities.

May you have happiness, and may you find it making one another happy.
May you have love, and may you find it loving one another!

James Dillet Freeman

Readings for a religious ceremony

Marriage prayers

God of wonder and of joy: grace comes from you, and you alone are the source of life and love.
Without you, we cannot please you; without your love, our deeds are worth nothing.
Send your Holy Spirit, and pour into our hearts that most excellent gift of love, that we may worship you now with thankful hearts and serve you always with willing minds; through Jesus Christ our Lord. *Amen*

God our Father, from the beginning you have blessed creation with abundant life.
Pour out your blessings upon (name of bride) and (name of groom), that they may be joined in mutual love and companionship, in holiness and commitment to each other.
We ask this through our Lord Jesus Christ your Son, who is alive and reigns with you,
in the unity of the Holy Spirit, one God, now and for ever. *Amen*

Blessed are you, O Lord our God, for you have created joy and gladness, pleasure and delight, love, peace and fellowship.
Pour out the abundance of your blessing upon (name of bride) and (name of groom) in their new life together.
Let their love for each other be a seal upon their hearts and a crown upon their heads.
Bless them in their work and in their companionship; awake and asleep, in joy and in sorrow, in life and in death.
Finally, in your mercy, bring them to that banquet where your saints feast for ever in your heavenly home.
We ask this through Jesus Christ your Son, our Lord, who lives and reigns with you and the Holy Spirit, one God, now and for ever. *Amen*

The Lord's Prayer

Our Father, which art in heaven,
Hallowed be thy name;
Thy kingdom come;
Thy will be done;
On earth as it is in heaven.
Give us this day our daily bread.
And forgive us our trespasses,
As we forgive those who trespass against us.
And lead us not into temptation;
But deliver us from evil.
For thine is the kingdom,
The power and the glory,
For ever and ever. *Amen*

Love, joy, understanding, friendship, courage...

In joining your lives may God grant you both...
Love... to afford each other a special quality of time together.
Joy... in the accomplishments of one another.
Understanding... that your interests and desires will not always be the same.
Friendship... based on mutual trust.
Courage... to speak of a misunderstanding and to work on a solution before the setting of the sun.
Compassion... to comfort each other in pain and sorrow.
Foresight... to realise rainbows follow rainy days.
Imagination... to keep with you part of the child you used to be.
Mirth... from your sense of humour.
Awareness... to live each day with the knowledge that there is no promise of tomorrow.
May God bless you and keep you in the palm of his hand. *Amen*

Readings for a religious ceremony

Gracious God, richly bless…

Gracious God, richly bless (name of bride) and (name of groom) in the promises that they have made to each other. Grant that the courtesies, the thoughtfulness, and the self giving which already
have laid the foundation for their love, build the home which is raised on it.
May they be loyal and engaging companions to each other, and may they be loving and wise parents.

And in this world where there is much disillusion and disappointment… where love brings delight and also wounding in the frailty of our ways… make them a visible symbol of the love that does not wane when the evening comes but is fresh with each new day.

And as you bless this special couple this day, bless each union represented here.
Forgive us where we have not been good news and glad days for each other. Perfect our imperfect love with the joy that comes from above, and may we grow ourselves and grow in affirmation of the other.

May the Lord bless you and take care of you:
May the Lord be kind and gracious to you:
May the Lord look on you with favour and give you peace. *Amen*

For more inspiration, see website www.cofe.anglican.org.

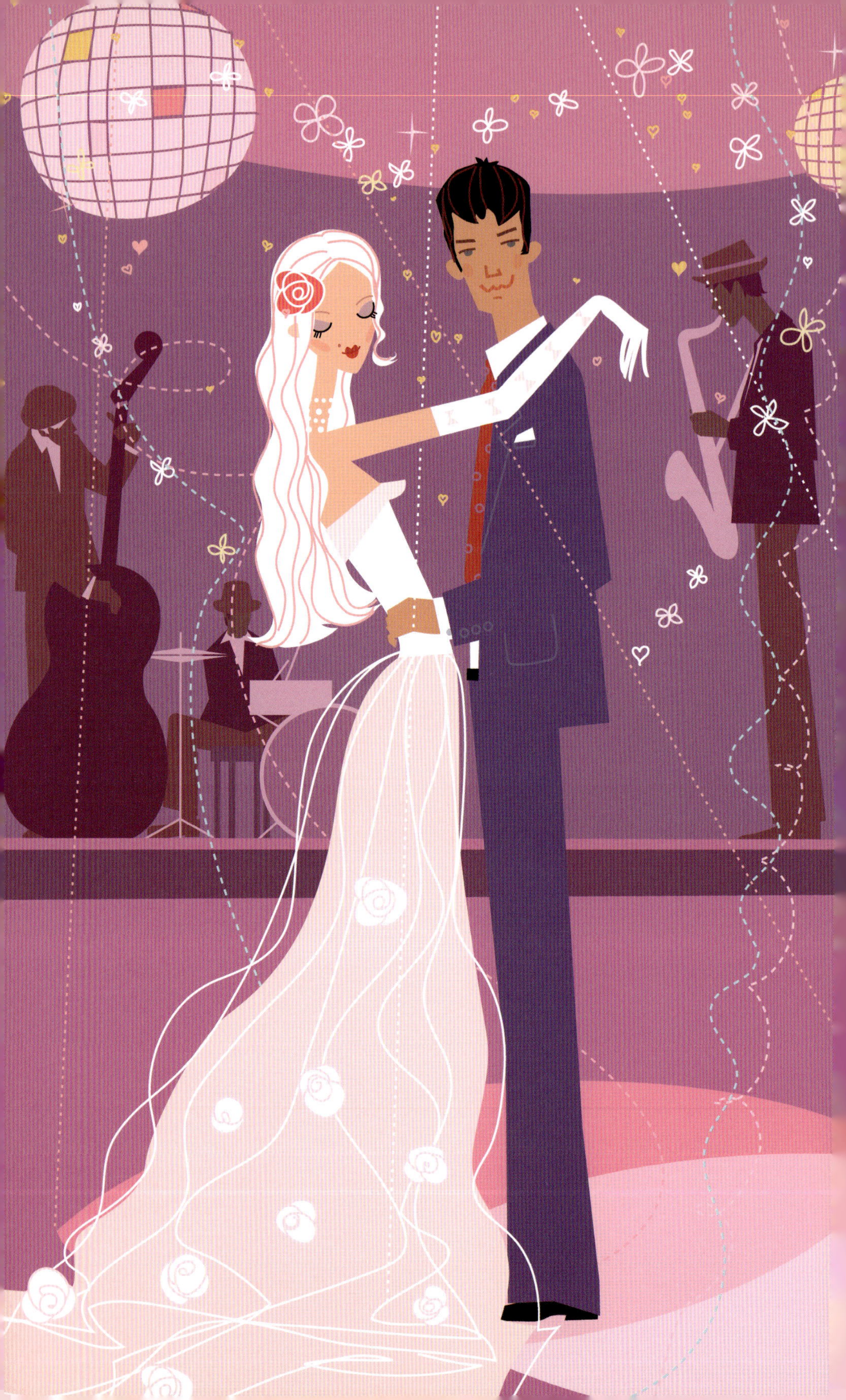

Chapter 6

Ceremony hymns & wedding music

The music you choose is the soundtrack to your wedding and plays an important role from the moment you walk into the ceremony to your first dance as man and wife. Wedding music is memories in the making, so choose it wisely.

Music is an essential part of any wedding and it can make or break the romantic mood. Start your musical journey by thinking about the moments during the day when music will be appropriate, and then about the type of music you want to play. If you are having a religious ceremony, it is usual to have an organist and/or choir providing the music. You may also like to think about a string quartet or perhaps a talented friend giving a short performance before you take your vows.

At a civil ceremony in a licensed building you can either have a live performance by a string quartet, harpist or jazz trio, or choose music on a CD playing in the background, although this does mean someone will have to be designated to turn it on, off, up and down at appropriate moments.

At a register office, when the ceremony is quick and informal, it is usual to have a CD player providing the music. Some couples have no music at all, although this does make it rather a dull affair for guests, particularly when they are sitting waiting for the arrival of the couple and during interludes like the signing of the register. Live music is an option at a register office, but you need to get agreement for this from the registrar. If they are busy and time is limited, they are likely to say no.

Ceremony music

Choosing music can be difficult; you know what you like and can probably recall snatches of all sorts of tunes – but you may not have a clue what they are called. This is where it is useful to get hold of a CD of classic wedding music to see if it contains any of your particular favourites. Your local library may have a CD lending facility and there are many inspirational music websites that play a few bars of many traditional songs to help you narrow down your options (see page 142).

You don't have to limit your choices to classical music, although remember that even a civil wedding is a solemn occasion and anything you choose must be suitably dignified. You and your intended may think that playing 'Bring your daughter to the slaughter' is amusing, but it is likely to result in a few raised eyebrows and perhaps not create the atmosphere you intended.

For a religious wedding, ask the advice of your minister. At a pre-wedding meeting the organist is usually more than happy to be on hand to play a few bars of popular themes to get you started. You may be allowed to play a romantic popular song as you walk up the aisle and then leave the church as man and wife, although some ministers will object, thinking it too informal, so do check everything first.

During a civil wedding at a licensed building you can usually pretty much choose what you like, although remember that none of the lyrics can contain religious references. Most couples go for a mixture of classics using 'Here comes the bride' to enter, something romantic like 'Love is all around' during the signing of the register and then leave to a suitably upbeat tune like 'Signed, sealed, delivered – I'm yours!'

At a register office there is less time to keep changing music, so it is probably wise to stick to one or two pieces of music that play quietly in the background throughout the ceremony.

Ceremony hymns & wedding music

If you want to use a song make sure you listen to the lyrics and understand what is being sung, and that it's appropriate for a wedding. For example, James Blunt's classic, '*You're Beautiful*' is often suggested, but the song is actually about a man who falls for a stranger and they are destined never to meet – it's more of a lament to what might have been than the romantic love of a wedding, and not really suitable at all. Take care, too, that if you choose a specific tune whoever is playing it knows which version you are thinking about. There is a wonderful story about a church organist breaking into 'Robin Hood, Robin Hood, riding through the glen…' as the bride walked up the aisle. What she actually had in mind when suggesting the theme from Robin Hood was 'Everything I do, I do it for you' by Bryan Adams, the theme from the *Prince of Thieves* movie!

Musical suggestions for the ceremony

The prelude: traditional options

'A Rose Is Gently Blooming,' Op 122, No 8, *Johannes Brahms*
Adagio for Strings, *Samuel Barber*
Air on a G String, *J S Bach*
'Aria, Bist du bei mir' (Be thou near me), BWV 508, *Johann S. Bach*
'Awake My Heart with Gladness,' *Flor Peeters*
Chorale in A Minor, Adagio, *Cesar Franck*
Concerto in D Minor, Adagio, *Tomaso Albinoni*
Largo from Xerxes, *George Frederic Handel*
'Perfect Love', *Sir Joseph Barnby*
'Nessun Dorma' from Turandot, *Giacomo Puccini*
Rhosymedre, *Ralph Vaughan Williams*
'Serenade' from String Quartet Op 3 No 5, *Franz Joseph Haydn*
'Serenade', *Franz Schubert*
'Sheep May Safely Graze', *J S Bach*
Sonata in G Minor for Flute and Organ, *George F Handel*
Toccata in E Minor, *Johann Pachelbel*
Violin Concerto in A, *Franz Joseph Haydn*

The prelude: contemporary options
'All I Ask Of You' from *Phantom of the Opera*, *Andrew Lloyd Webber*
'Angel Eyes', *Jim Brickman*
'Circle of Life', *Elton John* from *The Lion King*
'Evergreen', *Barbra Streisand*
'Loving You', *Kenny G*
'Truly', *Lionel Richie*
'Unchained Melody', *The Righteous Brothers*
'You and I', *Stevie Wonder*

The processional: traditional options
'Air' from Water Music Suite, *George F Handel*
'Bridal Chorus' (aka 'Here Comes The Bride') from Lohengrin, *Richard Wagner*
Canon in D, *Johann Pachelbel*
Procession of Joy, *Hal Hopson*
Romeo and Juliet Love Theme, *Tchaikovsky*
'Spring' from The Four Seasons, *Antonio Vivaldi*
Te Deum, *Marc-Antoine Charpentier*
The Prince of Denmark's March, *Jeremiah Clarke*
Toccata, from L'Orfeo, *Claudio Monteverdi*
Trumpet Tune, *Henry Purcell*
Trumpet Voluntary, *Jeremiah Clarke*
'Wedding March' from The Marriage of Figaro, *Wolfgang Amadeus Mozart*
'Winter,' Largo, from The Four Seasons, *Antonio Vivaldi*

The processional: contemporary options
'Have I Told You Lately', *Van Morrison*
'Sunrise, Sunset' from *Fiddler on the Roof*, *Sheldon Harnick & Jerry Bock*
'Take My Breath Away', *Berlin*
'The Look of Love', *Dionne Warwick & Burt Bacharach*
'The Vow', *Jeremy Lubbock*
'Wedding Processional' from *The Sound of Music*, *Rodgers & Hammerstein*
'Wind Beneath My Wings', *Bette Midler*
'You Are So Beautiful', *Joe Cocker*

Ceremony hymns & wedding music

The recessional: traditional options
'Allegro Maestoso' from Water Music Suite, *George F Handel*
Brandenburg Concerto No. 1, Allegro, *J S Bach*
'Coronation March' from Crown Imperial, *Sir William Walton*
'Hallelujah Chorus' from The Messiah, *George F Handel*
'Hornpipe' from Water Music Suite, *George F Handel*
'Ode to Joy', *Ludwig van Beethoven*
'Spring,' Allegro, from The Four Seasons, *Antonio Vivaldi*
'The Arrival of the Queen of Sheba', *George F Handel*
'Toccata' from Symphonie 5, Op 42, *Charles-Marie Widor*
'Triumphal March', *Edvard Grieg*
'Trumpet Tune and Bell Symphony,' *Henry Purcell*
'Variations on the Kanon by Pachelbel', *George Winston*
'Wedding March' from A Midsummer Night's Dream, *Felix Mendelssohn*

The recessional: contemporary options
'Beautiful Day', *U2*
'From This Moment On', *Cole Porter*
'Love is All Around', *Wet, Wet, Wet*
'Lovely Day', *Bill Withers*
'Oh! You Pretty Things', *David Bowie*
'Signed, Sealed, Delivered', *Stevie Wonder*
'Sunshine of My Life', *Stevie Wonder*
'The Long and Winding Road', *The Beatles*
'We've Only Just Begun', *The Carpenters*
'You To Me Are Everything', *Real Thing*

Interlude: traditional options

Adagio, *Felix Mendelssohn*

All Things Bright and Beautiful, traditional hymn

Andantino, *Cesar Franck*

Arioso, *J S Bach*

Ave Maria, *Franz Schubert*

Cantabile in B flat major, BI 84, *Frederic Chopin*

Clair de Lune, *Claude Debussy*

'Flower Duet' from Lakme, *Leo Delibes*

'Lento con tenerezza', *Enrique Granados*

'Love That Will Not Let Me Go', *Albert L Peace*

'Meditation' from Thais, *Jules Massenet*

Minuet from Berenice, *George F Handel*

Morning Has Broken, traditional hymn

'O mio babbino caro' from Gianni Schicchi, *Giacomo Puccini*

Romanza, *Ludwig van Beethoven*

Salut D'Amour, *Sir Edward Elgar*

Ceremony hymns & wedding music

Interlude: contemporary options
'A Simple Song', *Leonard Bernstein*
'Annie's Song', *John Denver*
'Benedictus', *Simon and Garfunkel*
'Grow Old With Me', *John Lennon*
'Kind and Generous', *Natalie Merchant*
'One Hand, One Heart', from *West Side Story, Leonard Bernstein & Stephen Sondheim*
'Take My Breath Away', *Tuck & Patti*
'Thank You', *Led Zeppelin*
'The Prayer', *Andreas Bocelli & Celine Dion*
'Through the Eyes of Love', *Carole Sager & Marvin Hamlisch*

Hymns for a church ceremony

Traditional hymns will always play a part in a religious wedding and there's nothing like the sound of voices singing an uplifting song, for example, 'All things bright and beautiful', to celebrate a marriage.

The traditional order of service includes spaces for two or three hymns, and where they come in the service can dictate whether they are quiet and reflective (at the beginning) to joyful and full of gusto (after you have said your vows). Discuss your choices with your minister who will be happy to help you with a short list.

It is advisable to choose classic, well-known hymns rather than anything more obscure that your guests may not know. There's nothing worse than a congregation not singing or mumbling unfamiliar words! If you are having a small wedding, paying to have the local church choir in attendance can be money well spent to create the right atmosphere.

If you want to reprint the words of the hymns in your order of service so your guests don't have to worry about hymn books, you may have to pay a small copyright fee (between £15 and £25), but again, your minister will advise on this. There will be no charge for just singing the hymns.

Traditional wedding hymns

The words of the first verse only are given, to jog your memory.

All things bright and beautiful

All things bright and beautiful,
All creatures great and small,
All things wise and wonderful,
The Lord God made them all.

At the name of jesus

At the name of Jesus
Every knee shall bow,
Every tongue confess Him,
King of Glory now.

I danced in the morning (lord of the dance)

I danced in the morning
When the world was begun,
And I danced in the moon
And the stars and the sun,
And I came down from heaven
And I danced on the earth,
At Bethlehem I had my birth.

Love divine, all loves excelling

Love divine, all loves excelling.
Joy to heaven, to earth come down.
Fix in us thy humble dwelling,
All thy faithful mercies crown.
Jesus, Thou art all compassion,
Pure unbounded love thou art.
Visit us with Thy salvation,
Enter every trembling heart.

The lord's my shepherd (Psalm 23)

The Lord's my shepherd; I'll not want.
He maketh me down to lie
In pastures green; He leadeth me
The quiet waters by.

Dear lord and father of mankind

Dear Lord and Father of mankind,
Forgive our foolish ways.
Re-clothe us in our rightful mind,
In purer lives thy service find,
In deeper reverence praise,
In deeper reverence praise.

Praise my soul, the king of heaven

Praise my soul, the King of Heaven,
To His feet thy tribute bring;
Ransomed, healed, restored, forgiven,
Who like me His praise would sing?
Praise Him, praise Him, praise Him, praise Him,
Praise the everlasting King.

Lead us, heavenly father, lead us

Lead us, Heavenly Father, lead us,
O'er the world's tempestuous sea.
Guard us, guide us, keep us, feed us,
For we have no help but thee.
Yet possessing every blessing
If our God the Father be.

All people that on earth do dwell

All people that on earth do dwell,
Sing to the Lord with cheerful voice.
Serve Him with joy, His praises tell.
Come now before Him and rejoice.

Immortal, invisible

Immortal, invisible, God only wise.
In light inaccessible, hid from our eyes.
Most blessed, most glorious
The ancient of days,
Almighty, victorious,
Thy great name we praise.

Musical options for the reception

Music continues to play an important role once you and your guests arrive at the wedding reception. Welcome everyone to the drinks party with live music played by a classical jazz trio, string quartet or harpist. The performance gives your guests something to enjoy as they have a glass of champagne and chat while you have your photographs taken. If your venue has a good sound system in the rooms you are using, it is perfectly acceptable to play a compilation CD of your favourite romantic tunes. Providing the room is fairly small, your own CD player will probably suffice as well.

The entertainment you provide as your guests are eating is up to your budget. Lots of couples have no music during the meal, but you could have piped or live music. Whatever you choose, make sure it is nothing too loud. Your guests want to chat while they eat, not be assailed by music that makes for strained conversation.

If you are continuing your reception into the evening and having dancing, again it is up to your musical tastes and your budget what you choose. A band capable of playing a wide range of songs is always good value for money, adding to atmosphere and taking requests from your guests as the evening progresses. A DJ is another good option. For anyone with a Scottish or Irish background, a ceilidh, a form

Ceremony hymns & wedding music

of country dancing, is always lots of fun, as is having a Western barn dance at a summer wedding. You'll need to hire a suitable band and a caller who shouts out instructions and generally helps those unfamiliar with the steps to keep up.

Whatever style of music you decide on, agree a play list of favourites (and music you hate) in advance. It's as well to include a wide range of classic disco tunes that most of your guests will know, as well as some up-to-date material. Play safe and go for the middle ground – the aim of the music is for the majority to get up and dance, and this usually only happens with the golden oldies!

The first dance

The first dance undertaken by the bride and groom is the traditional signal that the evening part of the reception is about to begin. All the guests gather around the dance floor to watch as the newlyweds glide (or shuffle) their way through a chosen song. The first dance music is usually something slow and romantic, although you can entertain your guests with something more upbeat if you think your dancing skills are up to it. Many couples these days invest in a few dance lessons before the wedding, which is money well spent if you know you've got two left feet. Fred and Ginger you may not be, but even one lesson will help you to look more polished!

Once the first dance has ended the rest of the guests are welcome to join the happy couple on the dance floor. At this point the bride usually dances with her father and the groom dances with the bride's mother.

First dance classics

'A Groovy Kind of Love', *Phil Collins*
'All the Way', *Frank Sinatra*
'Come Fly With Me', *Frank Sinatra*
'Could It Be Magic', *Barry Manilow*
'Devoted to You', *The Everly Brothers*
'Endless Love', *Diana Ross and Lionel Ritchie*
'I Can't Give You Anything But Love', *Louis Armstrong*
'I Got You, Babe', *Sonny and Cher*
'I Only Have Eyes for You', *Art Garfunkel*
'It Had To Be You', *Harry Connick Jr*
'Love Me Tender', *Elvis Presley*
'My Baby Just Cares for Me', *Nina Simone*
'My Eyes Adored You', *Frankie Valli*
'My Girl', *The Temptations*
'My Heart Will Go On', *Celine Dion (*from *Titanic)*
'Someone to Watch Over Me', *Barbra Streisand*
'The Best is Yet to Come', *Frank Sinatra*
'When I Fall in Love, *Nat King Cole*

Contemporary first dance songs

'A Whole New World', *Regina Belle and Peabo Bryson (*from *Aladdin)*
'Ain't No Stopping Us Now', *McFadden and Whitehead*
'Always and Forever', *Heatwave*
'Can You Feel the Love Tonight?', *Elton John (*from *The Lion King)*
'From This Moment On', *Shania Twain*
'Have I Told You Lately', *Van Morrison*
'(Everything I Do) I Do It For You', *Bryan Adams (*from *Robin Hood: Prince of Thieves)*
'It Must be Love', *Madness*
'Just the Two of Us', *Grover Washington Jr*
'Let's Get it On', *Marvin Gaye*
'Let's Stay Together', *Al Green*
'My Cherie Amour', *Stevie Wonder*
'On Bended Knee', *Boyz II Men*

Ceremony hymns & wedding music

'Slave to Love', *Bryan Ferry*
'Sweet Love', *Anita Baker*
'Take My Breath Away', *Berlin* (from *Top Gun*)
'Tonight I Celebrate My Love', *Roberta Flack and Peabo Bryson*
'Truly Madly Deeply', *Savage Garden*
'Wonderful Tonight', *Eric Clapton*
'You Lift Me Up', *Westlife*
'You Make Me Feel Brand New', *The Stylistics*
'Your Love is King', *Sade*
'Your Song', *Elton John*

Dance songs for the bride and her father

'A Whole New World', *Peabo Bryson and Regina Bell* (from *Aladdin*)
'Father's Eyes', *Amy Grant*
'Have I Told You Lately', *Rod Stewart*
'Hero', *Mariah Carey*
'Isn't She Lovely', *Stevie Wonder*
'My Girl', *The Temptations*
'The Way You Look Tonight', *Frank Sinatra*
'Unforgettable', *Natalie Cole*
'Wind Beneath My Wings', *Bette Midler*

Dance floor dynamite

Want everyone up and dancing? With this mixture you can't go wrong!

- *Abba*
- *Barry White*
- *The Beatles*
- *The Bee Gees*
- *Elvis Presley*
- *Frank Sinatra*
- *Gloria Gaynor*
- *Kylie Minogue*
- *Lionel Ritchie*
- *Madonna*
- *Michael Jackson*
- *Robbie Williams*
- *Rolling Stones*
- *Scissor Sisters*
- *Take That*
- *Tom Jones*
- *UB40*
- *Village People*

Dance songs for the groom and his mother

'A Song for Mama', *Boyz II Men*

'Because You Loved Me', *Celine Dion*

'Blessed', *Elton John*

'Greatest Love of All', *Whitney Houston*

'Have I Told You Lately', *Rod Stewart*

'I Will Always Love You', *Whitney Houston* (from *The Bodyguard*)

'Wind Beneath My Wings', *Bette Midler*

Inspiration for music

Useful websites

www.classicalwedding.co.uk .... *References for and audio clips of suitable music.*
www.cyberhymnal.org .... *References for and audio clips of popular hymns.*
www.lyricsfreak.com .... *Lyrics of 100s of popular songs.*
www.wedalert.com .... *References for and audio clips of suitable music.*
www.weddingmusic.co.uk .... *References for and audio clips of suitable music.*
www.bbm.net/music-for-weddings.htm .... *Audio clips and inspiration.*
www.2-in-2-1.co.uk/weddings/wedmusic/ .... *Audio clips and inspiration.*
www.virtualsheetmusic.com/wedding.html .... *Sheet music to download.*

Musical inspiration reference books

Popular Love Songs & Wedding Music Easy Piano, by Dan Coates, Alfred Publishing Company, ISBN 978-0-757-93986-0

The Best Wedding Songs Ever, Hal Leonard Publishing Company, ISBN 978-0-634-07395-3

Musical inspiration: CDs

Website www.youandyourwedding.co.uk has two wedding music CDs with ideas for church and civil ceremonies, the contents of which are listed on pages 143-145. Both can be ordered direct from the website.

Ceremony hymns & wedding music

'You & Your Wedding' Bride's Guide to Wedding Music

Disc 1

1. 'Herz und Mund und Tat und Leben', BWV 147: Jesu, Joy of Man's Desiring (arr for organ)
2. 'Sheep may safely graze', BWV 208
3. Suite No 3 in D major, BWV 1068: 'Air on a G String'
4. String Quintet in E major, Op. 11, No 5: III Minuet (arr D Sosin)
5. The Four Seasons, Violin Concerto in F minor, Op 8, No 4, RV 297, Winter: II Largo
6. Gymnopédie No 1 (arr for flute and harp)
7. Orfeo ed Euridice: 'Dance of the Blessed Spirits' (arr for flute and harp)
8. Canon in D major
9. Lohengrin, Act III: Wedding March (arr for organ)
10. Trumpet Voluntary
11. Music for Royal Fireworks, HWV 351: Overture
12. Pictures at an Exhibition: Promenade
13. Te Deum, H 146: Prelude (arr for organ)
14. 'Zadok the Priest', HWV 258
15. Messiah, HWV 56: 'Hallelujah Chorus'
16. Solomon, HWV 67, Act III: Sinfonia, 'Arrival of the Queen of Sheba'
17. Trumpet Tune
18. 'Praise, my soul, the King of Heaven'
19. 'Immortal, Invisible'
20. 'Dear Lord and Father of Mankind'
21. 'Jesus Christ the Apple Tree'

Disc 2

1. Cantique de Jean Racine, Op 11
2. Vesperae solennes de confessore, K 339: Laudate Dominum
3. Ave verum corpus, K 618
4. Panis angelicus
5. The blue bird

6. Ellen's Gesang III ('Ave Maria!'), Op. 56, No. 6, D. 839, 'Hymne an die Jungfrau'
7. Requiem, Op 48: 'Pie Jesu'
8. Sicilienne, Op 78 (arr for flute and harp)
9. Thais, Act II: Meditation (trans by M P Marsick)
10. The Four Seasons: Violin Concerto in E major, Op 8, No 1, RV 269, 'Spring': I Allegro
11. Samson, HWV 57, Act III: 'Let the Bright Seraphim'
12. VI Air 02:01
13. IX Hornpipe
14. Organ Symphony No 5 in F minor
15. Crown Imperial – Coronation March
16. Jubilate Deo
17. A Midsummer Night's Dream

'You & Your Wedding' A Bride's Guide to Music For Civil Ceremonies

Disc 1

1. Canon in D major
2. Lohengrin, Act III Scene 1: Treulich gefuhrt, 'Bridal Chorus', 'Wedding Chorus' (arr for organ)
3. Suite in D major: IV. The Prince of Denmark's March, 'Trumpet Voluntary'
4. Music for the Royal Fireworks, HWV 351: I Overture
5. Pictures at an Exhibition (arr Ravel): I Promenade
6. Music for the Royal Fireworks, HWV 351: IV 'La rejouissance'
7. Solomon, HWV 67, Act III: Sinfonia, 'Arrival of the Queen of Sheba'
8. Overture (Suite) No 2 in B minor, BWV 1067: VII Badinerie
9. The Four Seasons: Violin Concerto in E major
10. The Indian Queen, Z. 630: Trumpet Tune
11. Le nozze di Figaro (The Marriage of Figaro), K 492: Overture
12. Tambourin
13. Lyric Pieces, Book 8, Op 65: No 6, 'Wedding Day at Troldhaugen'
14. Water Music: Suite No 1 in F major, HWV 348: IX Hornpipe
15. Symphony No 5 in F minor, Op 42, No 1: V Toccata 0

Ceremony hymns & wedding music

16 Crown Imperial (Coronation March)
17 Serenade No 13 in G major, K 525, 'Eine kleine Nachtmusik': I
18 Allegro
19 A Midsummer Night's Dream, Op 61: Wedding March (arr for organ)

Disc 2

1   Overture (Suite) No 3 in D major, BWV 1068: II Air, 'Air on a G String'
2   String Quintet in E major, Op 11, No 5 (G 275): III Minuetto
3   The Four Seasons: Violin Concerto in F minor, Op 8, No 4, RV 297, 'Winter': II Largo
4   Gymnopédie No 1 (arr for flute and harp)
5   Orfeo ed Euridice, Act II: 'Dance of the Blessed Spirits' (arr for flute and harp)
6   'Auf Flugeln des Gesanges' (On Wings of Song), Mendelssohn (from Op 34, No 2) S547/R217, No 1
7   Arabesque No 1 (arr for flute and harp)
8   Bagatelle in A minor, 'Fur Elise'
9   8 Part Songs, Op 119: No 3, 'The Bluebird'
10 Sicilienne, Op 78 (arr for flute and harp)
11 Thais, Act II: Meditation (arr for violin and piano)
12 Water Music: Suite No 1 in F major, HWV 348: VI Air
13 Suite bergamasque: No 3, 'Clair de Lune'
14 Le Carnaval des animaux (Carnival of the Animals): XIII 'Le cygne' (The Swan)
15 Carmen, Act III: Entr'acte (Intermezzo) (arr for flute and harp)
16 Cello Suite No 1 in G major, BWV 1007: I Prelude 0
17 Salut d'amour (Liebesgruss), Op 12 (arr for flute and harp)
18 Pavane, Op 50 (arr for guitar and orchestra)

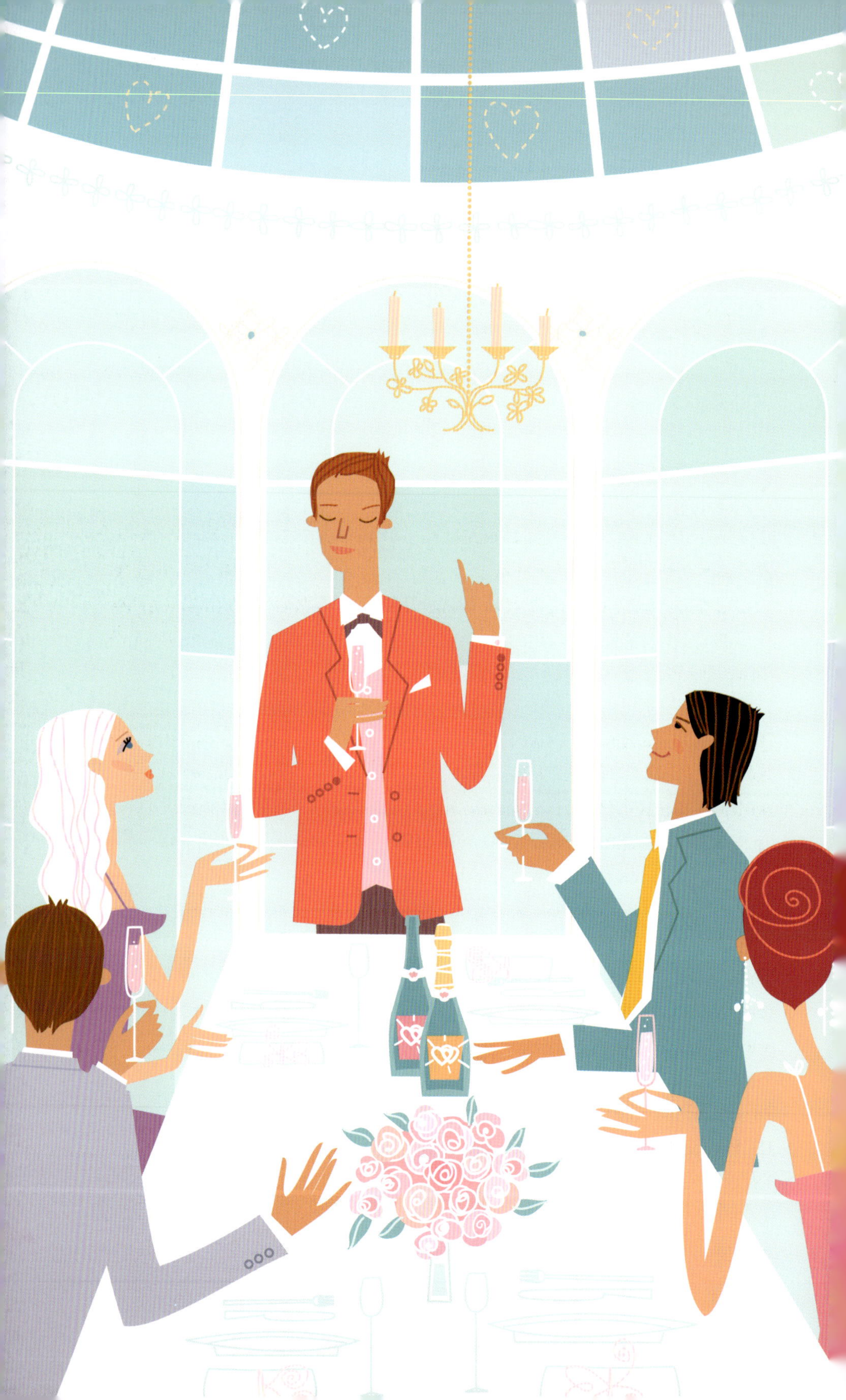

Chapter 7

Weddings speeches & toasts

All weddings include a mixture of speeches and toasts, meaningful moments delivered by members of the main bridal party offering thanks and good wishes to the happy couple, the parents and guests at the reception.

The wedding ceremony is not the only time when heartfelt words have an important role to play; the speeches at the reception also offer an opportunity to express good wishes, offer thanks to major role players and generally to entertain the guests. The speeches and toasts can often be the most memorable (and tear-jerking) part of the whole day. No pressure, then!

Speeches traditionally take place once the food is over and before the cake is cut and the coffee served. However, if nerves are in danger of ruining the reception for those concerned, it is perfectly acceptable for the speeches to be made before the meal begins allowing everyone to go on and enjoy the food. The usual running order for speeches is the bride's father followed by the groom (and perhaps the bride) and ends with the best man.

Not everyone is happy to speak in public and you need to reassure anyone expected to make a dreaded wedding speech that an Oscar-winning performance, whilst fabulous, is not expected. Sincerity, with the odd funny anecdote if they can manage it, will suffice.

The most important thing to remember is that all speakers need to speak slowly and clearly, projecting their voices so that the guests at the back of the room can hear. Ask your groom, dad or best man to practise beforehand with an impartial friend on hand to give an honest appraisal if he is mumbling or racing his words.

If the venue room is large, a microphone may be provided, in which case the speaker should take a moment before the reception starts to familiarise themselves on how it works – and how loud to speak – they don't want to deafen the guests!

Who says what?

Each of the main speakers has a traditional list of thanks to offer as part of his speech. This is usually said before the speaker adds anecdotes and stories of their own. Each speech ends with a toast.

The father of the bride
- Thanks the guests for coming.
- Says a few heart-warming words about his wonderful daughter and how pleased he is to be welcoming the groom into the family.
- Proposes a toast to the happy couple and their future happiness.

The groom
- Thanks the father of the bride for his speech and the toast.
- Says something meaningful about how happy he is to be married to his beautiful new wife.
- Gives out thank-you gifts to the best man, ushers, bridesmaids, both mothers and anyone else who has helped out.
- Proposes a toast to the bridesmaids.

The bride
- Has no set words to say but usually speaks with or just after the groom.
- Offers her thanks to parents and to guests for coming.
- Has a great opportunity to tell everyone how much she loves her new husband, maybe reciting an appropriate poem or even singing a song (basically anything that will mildly embarrass the groom!).

Wedding speeches & toasts

The best man
- Thanks the groom on behalf of the bridesmaids and other attendants for his kind words.
- Launches into five minutes of banter that largely revolves around anecdotes about the groom in his past life, maybe involving props or even a short film.
- Proposes a toast to the bride and groom.

Writing a speech out on paper and aiming to read it out word for word is never a good idea. You'll end up looking down the whole time and it is much more likely you'll race your words. Instead, suggest that anyone making a speech puts key phrases on to cue cards. Once they've practised a few times, they won't need reminding of every word, just prompts to make sure nothing important gets forgotten. Cue cards need to be numbered so they are kept in the right order.

Father of the bride
speech template

Good afternoon, ladies and gentlemen.

I'm delighted to welcome you all here today to celebrate the marriage between my beautiful daughter *(name of bride)* and *(name of groom)*.

Thank you all so much for joining our families on this wonderful occasion. *(Insert thoughts on the ceremony, what it has meant to the family.)*

I have to take a moment and say how beautiful my daughter looks today. I have never seen her looking so radiant. *(Name of groom)*, you are a lucky man. You had better look after her or you'll be answering to me!

(Insert funny/touching story about the groom asking permission to marry daughter or feelings when they announced their engagement.)

I would also like to offer you both a few words of wisdom on the subject of enjoying a happy marriage. For a start, she's always right and you are always wrong! *(A funny or touching anecdote on a successful marriage, children, money and so on.)*

Just before I sit down, I would also like to thank our fabulous venue today. I hope you all enjoyed the wonderful meal. Congratulations to *(name of caterer/venue)*. Your team has done an amazing job and everything was delicious.

Now all that remains is for me to ask you all to be up-standing to toast the future health and happiness of *(names of the bride and groom):* the bride and groom.

(Introduce the groom to give his speech.)

Wedding speeches & toasts

Groom
speech template

Good afternoon, ladies and gentleman. I've been told that this is one of the only times in a man's life when he can be in the company of his wife and mother-in-law and not be interrupted *(pause)* I may be here some time! *(Or similar amusing anecdote.)*

I'd like to take this opportunity to thank *(name of father-in-law)* for his kind words. I am delighted to be joining the *(name of wife's family)* family and rest assured I will treasure *(name of wife)* forever. *(Funny story about asking father-in-law's permission to marry his daughter, if appropriate.)*

May I join *(name of father-in-law)* in thanking everyone for being here today. *(Make an observation about the day so far, what it has meant to you.)*

Before I say thank you to our wonderful bridesmaids, I would just like to say a few words about my beautiful new wife. *(Insert heartfelt, funny story about meeting your wife.)*

I would now like to propose a toast to the bridesmaids. *(Each bridesmaid can be asked up in turn to receive a small gift.)*

I would also like to say a huge thank you and propose a toast to our parents. Your love and support means the world to us. *(Toast the bride's parents, naming them, then the groom's parents. This may also be an appropriate time to mention 'absent friends', including a deceased friend or relative.)*

Finally, I would like to say thank you to my best man – although I may be reconsidering this once he has given his speech! *(Introduce the best man to give his speech.)*

Bride
speech template

Good afternoon, everyone. I can tell by the look on *(groom's name)*'s face that me making a speech has come as something of a shock – but I couldn't let this moment pass without sharing my feelings on this very special occasion.

I want to tell you, in front of all our family and friends, just how much I love you. It goes without saying that you are the luckiest man in the world to have married me – and I am the luckiest girl to have become your wife today.

I knew from the first minute I set eyes on you that we were destined to be together and that with you by my side nothing is impossible. I cannot wait to start our new married life and look forward to every adventure with anticipation and joy. *(Insert amusing anecdote about how you met, memorable occasion during your relationship etc, if appropriate)*

I would also like to add my heartfelt thanks to everyone for joining us here today. *(Name of groom)* and I are truly touched by all your love and good wishes. At this point I could do something hideously embarrassing, like bursting into song, but you'll be glad to hear I haven't drunk nearly enough champagne for that. Instead, please join me as I propose a toast to my wonderful groom, my one true love. The groom.

Wedding speeches & toasts

Best man
speech template

Ladies and gentlemen, I would like to thank *(name of groom)* on behalf of the bridesmaids for his *(kind/brief/heartfelt)* words. I agree that they all look *(lovely/sweet/drunk)*. I was *(honoured/shocked/confused)* when *(name of groom)* asked me to be his best man and presumed everyone else had said no. Even *(name of least likely guest)* said he had joined the *(Foreign Legion/a monastery)* and couldn't possibly oblige. So here I am, and where do I start?

I first met *(name of groom)* when we were both *(at school/in the pub/at reform school)* when his nickname was *(if none, make one up)* and we immediately became *(great friends/drinking buddies/rivals)*. Since that time things have got progressively *(better/worse)*. We have been through many things together, including *(puberty/drinking/partying)* and most memorable of all was when we were *(age)* and *(name of groom)* got into *(amusing anecdote)*.

Unfortunately, things didn't get much better either, when *(number)* years later he also *(amusing anecdote)*.

And at last we come to the stag night. From what I can recall, it all started off sedately but ended up in drunken debauchery *(story from stag night)* when *(name of groom)* ended up *(naked/in jail/tied to a lamppost)*.

It was *(years)* ago when *(name of groom)* met *(name of bride)*, the *(best/worst/we'll come back to you)* thing that ever happened to him. It was *(love/lust)* at first sight. It took *(name of groom)* *(number of days/weeks/months/years)* to pluck up the courage to ask *(name of bride)* to go *(on a date/to bed)* and the rest is history.

I ask you now to raise your glasses and join me in a toast to the bride and groom.

To Mr and Mrs (name). May their life together bring them much happiness.

Wedding toasts

A toast is a chance for everyone to raise their glasses and offer congratulations, thanks and good wishes. Most of the main speeches end with a short toast, but other friends and family not involved in giving a speech may also like to take the opportunity to say a few words. Toasts are often made by the father of the groom, the chief bridesmaid and perhaps a long-standing family friend who is renowned for his or her wise words.

If you are thinking of having a moment for general toasts, a good time is after the best man's speech and before the cake cutting ceremony. Just be watchful that it doesn't turn into an 'open mic' session with too many people thinking this is their chance to get up and take a turn. The best man should be charged with cutting the toasts short before they start to lose their charm!

The recipient or recipients of a toast generally raise their glass in acknowledgment of the kind words, but don't drink. The recipient can remain seated or sometimes stands up – although the bride and groom may get a little tired of bobbing up and down if the toasts are lengthy. Make sure your caterers have gone around charging glasses before the speeches, so that the toasting isn't done with empty glasses. A glass of champagne is the traditional toast drink for the main bridal toasts, but any drink is acceptable.

Toasts can be as simple as: 'Please raise your glasses and join me in toasting the happy couple, may all your problems be little ones. The bride and groom!'

Quotations that make good toasts

The great secret of a successful marriage is to treat all disasters as incidents and none of the incidents as disasters.
Sir Harold Nicholson

A successful marriage requires falling in love many times over, always with the same person.
Mignon McLaughlin

Wedding speeches & toasts

Love, be true to her; life, be dear to her;
Health, stay close to her; joy, draw near to her;
Fortune, find what you can do for her,
Search your treasure-house through and through for her.
Follow her footsteps the wide world over –
And keep her husband always her lover.
Anna Lewis

If you want something to make everyone smile, try:

To keep your marriage brimming with love in the wedding cup,
Whenever you're wrong admit it; whenever you're right, shut up.
Ogden Nash

A family starts with a young man falling in love with a girl.
No superior alternative has been found.
Winston Churchill

You don't marry one person; you marry three – the person you think they are, the person they are, and the person they are going to become as a result of being married to you.
Richard Needham

Coming together is a beginning;
Keeping together is progress;
Working together is success.
Henry Ford

Don't smother each other. No one can grow in shade.
Leo Buscaglia

For you see, each day I love you more,
Today more than yesterday and less than tomorrow.
Rosemonde Gerard

I love thee to the depth and breadth and height my soul can reach.
Elizabeth Barrett Browning

Whatever our souls are made of, his and mine are the same.
Emily Brontë

Love is not a matter of counting the years, it is making the years count.
Love is the master key that opens the gates of happiness.
Oliver Wendell Holmes

One advantage of marriage is that, when you fall out of love with him or he falls out of love with you, it keeps you together until you fall in again.
Judith Viorst

Marriage is an alliance entered into by a man who can't sleep with the window shut, and a woman who can't sleep with the window open.
George Bernard Shaw

The sum which two married people owe to one another defies calculation. It is an infinite debt, which can only be discharged through eternity.
Johann Wolfgang von Goethe

Love is an ideal thing, marriage is a real thing.
Johann Wolfgang von Goethe

What counts in making a happy marriage is not so much how compatible you are, but how you deal with incompatibility.
Leo Tolstoy

Love at first sight is easy to understand; it's when two people have been looking at each other for a lifetime that it becomes a miracle.
Sam Levenson

Wedding speeches & toasts

Marriage is the weaving together of families, of two souls with their individual fates and destinies, of time and eternity – everyday life married to the timeless mysteries of the soul.
Sir Thomas Moore

The most happy marriage I can picture would be the union of a deaf man to a blind woman.
Samuel Taylor Coleridge

Marriage resembles a pair of shears, so joined that they cannot be separated; often moving in opposite directions, yet always punishing anyone who comes between them.
Sydney Smith

When two people are under the influence of the most violent, most insane, most delusive and most transient of passions, they are required to swear that they will remain in that excited, abnormal, and exhausting condition continuously until death do them part.
George Bernard Shaw

There is no more lovely, friendly and charming relationship, communion or company than a good marriage.
Martin Luther

May there always be work for your hands to do.
May your purse always hold a coin or two.
May the sun always shine on your windowpane.
May a rainbow be certain to follow each rain.
May the hand of a friend always be near you.
May God fill your heart with gladness to cheer you.
Traditional Irish toast

There is only one happiness in life, to love and be loved.
George Sand

There is nothing nobler or more admirable than when two people who see eye to eye keep house as man and wife, confounding their enemies and delighting their friends.
Homer

Remember, we all stumble, every one of us. That's why it's a comfort to go hand in hand.
Emily Kimbrough

Never marry for money, you can borrow it cheaper.
Scottish Proverb

Shared joy is a double joy; shared sorrow is half a sorrow.
Swedish Proverb

Simple suggestions for toasts

The toasts that follow are all traditional and, therefore, anonymous:

To the newlyweds. May 'for better or worse' be far better than worse.

May the most you ever wish for be the least you ever receive.

May the saddest day of your future be no worse than the happiest day of your past.

Love puts the fun in together, the sad in apart, and the joy in a heart.

Love is a symbol of eternity. It wipes out all sense of time, destroying all memory of a beginning and all fear of an end.

Love: a wildly misunderstood although highly desirable malfunction of the heart which weakens the brain, causes eyes to sparkle, cheeks to glow, blood pressure to rise and the lips to pucker.

Wedding speeches & toasts

**I dreamed of a wedding of elaborate elegance,
A church filled with family and friends.
I asked him what kind of wedding he wished for,
He said one that would make me his wife.**

Here's to the health of the happy pair;
May good luck follow them everywhere;
And may each of wedded bliss
Be always as sweet and joyous as this.

We are all a little weird and life's a little weird, and when we find someone whose weirdness is compatible with ours, we join up with them and fall in mutual weirdness and call it love.

No man is truly married until he understands every word his wife is not saying.

The most eloquent silence: that of two mouths meeting in a kiss.

Trip over love and you can get up. Fall in love and you fall forever.

The definition of a spouse: someone who'll stand by you through all the trouble you wouldn't have had if you'd stayed single.

Newlyweds become oldyweds, and oldyweds are the reasons that families work.

A happy man marries the girl he loves; a happier man loves the girl he marries.

Every mother generally hopes that her daughter will snag a better husband than she managed to do… but she's certain that her boy will never get as great a wife as his father did.

Every minute you spend angry with your partner is a waste of sixty seconds in which you could be enjoying yourselves.

You don't marry someone you can live with, you marry the person who you cannot live without.

Love is a symbol of eternity. It wipes out all sense of time, destroying all memory of a beginning and fear of an end.

Soul mates: two halves of the same soul joining together in life's journey.

If I could reach up and hold a star for every time you've made me smile, the entire evening sky would be in the palm of my hand.

When you meet someone who can cook and do housework, don't hesitate for a minute: marry him!

A toast to love and laughter, and happily ever after.

When a newly married couple smiles, everyone knows why. When a ten-year married couple smiles, everyone wonders why.

Toasts to the bride and groom

Here's to the groom with bride so fair.
And here's to the bride with groom so rare!

**I wish you health; I wish you wealth; I wish you gold in store;
I wish you heaven when you die, what could I wish you more?**

May you have many children,
And may they grow mature in taste
And healthy in colour
And as sought after
As the contents of this glass.
Traditional Irish toast

Wedding speeches & toasts

**May you have warm words on a cold evening,
a full moon on a dark night
and the road downhill all the way to your door.**
Traditional Irish toast

Here's to the bride and groom. May their happiness last forever and may we be fortunate enough to continue being a part of it.

Traditional toasts to the bride and groom

A toast to sweethearts.
May all sweethearts become married couples,
And may all married couples remain sweethearts.

**Here's to the new husband
And here's to the new wife
May they remain lovers
For all of their life.**

My love for you is a journey;
Starting at forever,
And ending at never.

Love one another and be happy. It's as simple and as difficult as that.

My greatest wish for the two of you is that through the years your love will deepen and grow, that years from now you will look back on this day as the day you loved each other the least.

May for 'better or worse' be far better than worse.

May your love be as endless as your wedding rings.

Toasts from the bride and groom to their guests

Among those whom I like, I can find no common denominator, but among those whom I love, I can; all of them make me laugh.
W H Auden

May our house always be too small to hold all our friends.
Myrtle Reed

To friendship, the only cement that will hold the world together.
Traditional

Here's to Eternity – may we spend it in as good company as this night finds us.
Traditional

It is written that when children find love, parents find true joy. Here's to your joy and ours, from this day and forever more.

Traditional toasts made by the father of the bride

Wise words for the groom: the most effective way of remembering your wedding anniversary is to forget it once.

Here's to the lasses we've loved, my lad
Here's to the lips we've pressed;
For of kisses and lasses
Like liquor in glasses,
The last is always the best.
Traditional Scottish toast

Wedding speeches & toasts

Toasts from the bride to her groom

Love me, sweet with all thou art
Feeling, thinking, seeing,
Love me in the lightest part
Love me in full being.
Elizabeth Barrett Browning

I have spread my dreams under your feet;
Tread softly, because you tread on my dreams.
W B Yeats

Traditional toasts from the bride to her groom

My love for you is a journey;
Starting at forever,
And ending at never.

Here's to the man that's good and sweet,
Here's to the man that's true.
Here's to the man that rules my heart,
In other words, here's to you.

I love you more than yesterday and less than I will tomorrow.

May we love as long as we live,
And live as long as we love.

Toasts from the groom to his bride

Your words are my food, your breath my wine.
You are everything to me.
Sarah Bernhardt

Traditional toasts from the groom to his bride

Because I love you truly,
Because you love me, too,
My greatest happiness
Is sharing life with you.

To my bride. She knows all about me and loves me just the same.

I have known many, liked not a few. Loved only one, I toast to you.

Toasts by the best man

My heart to you is given:
Oh, do give yours to me;
We'll lock them up together,
And throw away the key.
Frederick Saunders

Traditional toasts by the best man

May you be poor in misfortunes and rich in blessings,
Slow to make enemies and quick to make friends,
And may you know nothing but happiness from this day forward.
Traditional Irish toast

A health to you,
A wealth to you,
And the best that life can give to you.
May fortune still be kind to you.
And happiness be true to you.
And life be long and good to you.
This is a toast of all your friends to you.
Traditional Irish toast

Wedding speeches & toasts

Here's a toast to your new bride who has everything a girl could want in her life, except for good taste in men!

**May your hands be forever clasped in friendship
And your hearts joined forever in love.**

Here's to the bride. May your hours of joy be as numerous as the petals on your bouquet.
Here's to the groom, a man who keeps his head though loses his heart.

Toasts to the bridesmaids

I have a dozen healths to drink to these fair ladies.
William Shakespeare, from Henry VIII

Keats says, 'A thing of beauty is a joy forever.' Here's to these beautiful bridesmaids.
Anon

Traditional toasts to the assembled guests

Here's to eternity – may we spend it in as good company as this night finds us.

May the friends of our youth be the companions of our old age.

It is around the table that friends understand
best the warmth of being together.
Italian proverb

**Let us toast the bride;
Let us toast the groom;
Let us toast the person that tied;
Let us toast every guest in the room.**

Toast to parents/grandparents

Let us raise our glasses, and then imbibe
To the splendid couple who founded this tribe.
Traditional

Toast to absent friends

Absent friends – though out of sight we recognise them with our glasses.
Traditional

Blessings

At a traditional reception, and especially those following a religious wedding, it is usual to offer a blessing and say grace before the meal. This can be performed by the minister or vicar if he or she is attending, the Master of Ceremonies, the father of the bride or the best man.

A traditional grace is:
For what we are about to receive, may the Lord make us truly thankful. Amen.

Other examples:
Bless us, O Lord and these Thy gifts which we have received out of Thy bounty, through Christ our Lord. *Amen*
Traditional Catholic grace

Bless, O Lord, this food to our use, and us to Thy service, and make us ever needful of the needs of others, in Jesus' name. *Amen*
Traditional Protestant grace

Blessed are You, Adonai our God, Source of the Universe, who brings forth bread from the earth. Amen.
Traditional Jewish blessing over challah bread

Your notes

Order of service
religious ceremony

This is the traditional order of service for you to complete as you plan your ideal ceremony.

Prelude (as guests are seated) ....

Musical accompaniment ....

Performed by ....

Entrance of the bride ....

Musical accompaniment ....

Performed by ....

Introduction by the minister ....

Hymn 1 ....

The Marriage Ceremony ....

Prayers ....

Reading 1 ....

Reader ....

Hymn 2 ....

Order of service

Reading 2 ....

Reader ....

Optional musical performance..

Chosen music...

Performer(s)...

Conclusion of the marriage ceremony ....

Signing of the register..

Musical accompaniment ....

Performed by...

Recessional (exit of the bride and groom) ....

Musical accompaniment ....

Performed by...

Your notes..

....

....

....

Order of service
civil ceremony

This is the traditional order of service for you to complete as you plan your ideal ceremony.

Prelude (as guests are seated) ....

Musical accompaniment ....

Performed by ....

Entrance of the bride ....

Musical accompaniment ....

Performed by ....

Introduction by the officiant ....

Reading 1 ....

Reader ....

The marriage ceremony ....

Reading 2 ....

Reader ....

Optional musical performance or soloist ....

Order of service

Chosen music ....

Performer(s) ....

Conclusion of the marriage ceremony ....

Signing of the register ....

Musical accompaniment ....

Performed by ....

Recessional (exit of the bride and groom) ....

Musical accompaniment ....

Performed by ....

Your notes ....

....

....

....

....

....

....

Acknowledgements

The sanctity of marriage (page 105)
Extracted from 'A Wedding Sermon from a Prison Cell', May 1943; in Dietrich Bonhoeffer, *Letters and Papers from Prison*, The Enlarged Edition, 1971, pp 42f. reprinted by permission of SCM Press in the UK and Simon and Schuster Inc. in the USA.

The depth of love (page 64)
Extracted from *Women Who Love Too Much* by Robin Norwood, published in the UK by Arrow and in the US by Penguin Group (USA) Inc. Reprinted by permission of The Random House Group Ltd in the UK and Penguin Group (USA) Inc. in the USA.

What every woman knows sooner or later (pages 78–79)
Extracted from a book entitled *Candy Is Dandy – The Best of Ogden Nash* by Ogden Nash with an Introduction by Anthony Burgess. Copyright © 1934 by Ogden Nash. Reprinted by permission of Andre Deutsch and Curtis Brown, Ltd.

'Til death do us part (page 122)
Extracted from *Marriage Is a Balance Beam* by Carol D Bos, 1996. Reprinted by permission of Baker Books, a division of Baker Publishing Group.

On love and relationships (page 115)
Extracted from *A Gift from the Sea* by Anne Morrow Lindbergh, published by Chatto & Windus. Reprinted by permission of The Random House Group Ltd.

Index

References in italic indicate titles of readings

A

All people that on earth do dwell 138
All things bright and beautiful 136
Apache Marriage Blessing (Anon) 45
At the name of Jesus 136

B

Baptist ceremonies 18
beauty of love, The (Anon) 43
Berry, Wendell: *The path of marriage* 102
Bible readings
  Clothed in salvation 89
  The constancy of Ruth 93
  For everything a season 87
  God creates woman for man 86
  God is our refuge and strength 91
  A good wife 88
  His steadfast love endures forever 90
  I am the vine and you are the branches 96
  I lift up my eyes to the hills 92
  I will make you my wife 89
  Let love be genuine 97
  Let us sing to the Lord 90
  Love 94
  Love is as strong as death 93
  Love one another as I have loved you 97
  May God be gracious 92
  Promise of hope 89
  Put on love which binds everything together in harmony 94
  The Sermon on the Mount 96
  Two are better than one 87
  Wives submit to your husbands . . . 95

Blessing for a marriage (Freeman) 124
blessings 166
Blumenthal, Michael: *A marriage* 53
Bonhoeffer, Dietrich: *The sanctity of marriage* 105
Bos, Carol D: *'Til death us do part* 122
Bowen, Bud Henry: *A marriage prayer* 113
Bradstreet, Anne: *To my dear loving husband* 107
Brown, Pam: *Marriage is the beginning of an enterprise* 108
Browning, Elizabeth Barrett: *How do I love thee?* 117
Burns, Robert: *A red, red rose* 63
Byron, Lord George *She walks in beauty* 69

C

Cavendish, William: *There is no happier life but in a wife* 116
Chinese poem, A (Anon) 50
Church of England ceremonies 18
Clare, John: *First love* 65
Colgan, Dorothy R: *I promise* 59
colour of my love, The (Foster and Janov) 68
Cooper, Rachel Elizabeth: *Today I married my best friend* 51
Curtis, Stephen Chapman: *I will be here* 67

Index

D
Dante: *On love* 114
Dear lord and father of mankind 137
dedication to my wife, A (Eliot) 49
depth of love, The (Norwood) 64
Diamant, Anita: *The seven blessings* 99
Dove poem (Anon) 61
Dugdale, Pamela: *Our great adventure* 48

E
Eliot, T S: *A dedication to my wife* 49

F
Ferrine, Paul: *Peace and love* 120
first day, The (Rossetti) 73
First love (Clare) 65
Fordham, Mary Weston: *Marriage* 47
Foster, David (with Arthur Janov): *The colour of my love* 68
Foundations of marriage (Hill) 57
Freeman, James Dillet: *Blessing for a marriage* 124

G
Gibran, Kahlil: *Marriage* 103
good wedding cake, A (Anon) 66
graces 166
Gracious God, richly bless . . . (prayer) 127

H
Hand of the bride and groom (Anon) 60
Hill, Regina: *Foundations of marriage* 57
Hindu ceremonies 19
How do I love thee? (E B Browning) 117
Hugo, Victor: *You can give without loving* 42
Humanist ceremonies 14, 20
hymns 135–8

I
I knew that I had been touched by love (Anon) 62
I promise (Colgan) 59
I will be here (Curtis) 67
Immortal, invisible 138
Intimacy and fidelity in marriage (E and J Whitehead) 110
Irish blessing (Anon) 112

J
Janov, Arthur (with David Foster): *The colour of my love* 68
Jewish ceremonies 20, 98–9

K
key to love, The (Anon) 74
Kuan Tao-Sheng: *Married love* 52

L
Lawrence, D H: *Learning to love* 123
Lead us, heavenly father, lead us 137
Learning to love (Lawrence) 123
legalities for marriage 11
Lewis, C S: *Love and being in love* 119
Lindbergh, Anne Morrow: *On love and relationships* 115
Lord of the dance 136
lord's my shepherd, The 137
Lord's Prayer, The 126
Love, joy, understanding, friendship, courage (prayer) 126
Love and age (Peacock) 70–1
Love and being in love (Lewis) 119
Love divine, all loves excelling 136
Love's philosophy (Shelley) 118

M
marriage, A (Blumenthal) 53
marriage, A (Twain) 104
Marriage advice (Wells) 110
Marriage (Fordham) 47
Marriage (Gibran) 103

Index

Marriage is . . . (Anon) 104
Marriage is a commitment (Anon) 100
Marriage is one long conversation (Stevenson) 102
Marriage is the beginning of an enterprise (Brown) 108
Marriage joins two people in the circle of love (O'Neill) 101
Marriage lends permanence . . . (Schnell) 77
Marriage morning (Tennyson) 72
marriage prayer, A (Bowen) 113
Married love (Kuan Tao-Sheng) 52
marrying abroad 14–15
Methodist ceremonies 19
microphones 36
music
  for ceremonies
    choosing 129–31
    hymns 135–8
    suggestions 131–5
  for receptions 138–45
    bride and her father 141
    dance floor dynamite 141
    first dance 139–41
    groom and his mother 142
Muslim ceremonies 20
My true love (Sydney) 121

N

Nash, Ogden: *What almost every woman knows sooner or later* 78–9
Native American wedding ceremony, extract from (Anon) 44
Neruda, Pablo: *Sonnet LXIX* 41
Never marry but for love (Penn) 58
Nichols-Haining, Mari: *Why marriage?* 111
Norwood, Robin: *The depth of love* 64

O

On love and relationships (Lindbergh) 115
On love (Dante) 114
On your wedding day (Anon) 40
O'Neill, Edmund: *Marriage joins two people in the circle of love* 101
order of service 10–11, 31, 34
Our great adventure (Dugdale) 48

P

path of marriage, The (Berry) 102
Peace and love (Ferrine) 120
Peacock, Thomas Love: *Love and age* 70–1
Penn, William: *Never marry but for love* 58
Praise my soul, the king of heaven 137
prayers 125–7

Q

quotations
  moment of mirth 84
  sayings and proverbs 80–2
  for toasts 154–8
  views on marriage 76–7

R

readings
  choosing 33–4
  civil ceremonies 34, 39–83
  duration 33
  inspiration for 36–7
  making part of the ceremony 36
  religious ceremonies 34, 85–99
  who should give 35
red, red rose, A (Burns) 63
Reiser, Steven: *To my bride* 46
Roman Catholic ceremonies 18
Rossetti, Christina: *The first day* 73

Index

S

sanctity of marriage, The (Bonhoeffer) 105
Schnell, Johnathan: *Marriage lends permanence . . .* 77
seven blessings, The (Diamant) 99
Shakespeare, William: *Sonnet 116* 109
She walks in beauty (Byron) 69
Shelley, Percy Bysshe: *Love's philosophy* 118
Sonnet 116 (Shakespeare) 109
speeches 147–8
  best man 149, 153
  bride 148, 152
  father of bride 148, 150
  groom 148, 151
Stevenson, Robert Louis: *Marriage is one long conversation* 102
Sydney, Sir Phillip: *My true love* 121

T

Tennyson, Alfred Lord: *Marriage morning* 72
There is no happier life but in a wife (Cavendish) 116
These I can promise (Anon) 56
This day I married my best friend (Anon) 51
'Til death us do part (Bos) 122
To my bride (Reiser) 46
To my dear loving husband (Bradstreet) 107
toasts 154–60
  absent friends 166
  by best man 164–5
  to bride and groom 160–1
  by bride and groom to guests 162
  by bride to her groom 163
  to bridesmaids 165
  by father of the bride 162
  by groom to his bride 163–4
  to guests 165
  to parents/grandparents 166
Today I married my best friend (Cooper) 51
Tribal wish of the Iorquois (Anon) 44
True love (Anon) 54, 121
Twain, Mark: *A marriage* 104

V

vows 12, 17
  Baptist 18
  Church of England 18
  civil ceremonies 17, 21–30
  Hindu 19
  Humanist 20
  Jewish 20
  Methodist 19
  Muslim 20
  renewing 30–1
  Roman Catholic 18

W

walled garden, A (Anon) 106
Wedding day (Anon) 55
Wells, Jane: *Marriage advice* 110
What almost every woman knows sooner or later (Nash) 78–9
When you are old (Yeats) 75
Whitehead, Evelyn and James: *Intimacy and fidelity in marriage* 110
Why marriage? (Nichols-Haining) 111

Y

Yeats, W B: *When you are old* 75
You are my husband (Eskimo love song) 46
You can give without loving (Hugo) 42